Pi Beta Theta

Handbook of the Beta theta pi in the forty-eighth year of the

fraternity

Pi Beta Theta

**Handbook of the Beta theta pi in the forty-eighth year of the fraternity**

ISBN/EAN: 9783337268817

Printed in Europe, USA, Canada, Australia, Japan

Cover: Foto ©Andreas Hilbeck / pixelio.de

More available books at **www.hansebooks.com**

# HAND BOOK

## OF THE

# Beta Theta Pi

## in the forty-eighth year

### OF THE

# FRATERNITY.

MDCCCLXXXVI

# PREFACE.

In every part of the Hand-Book the point of departure is the opening of the convention held at Chicago in August, 1881. The point at which the book closes is the middle of April, 1886.

The lists of the members admitted within the period above described were first made up from the roll that is kept in the general secretary's office and were then submitted to the chapters for revision. The addresses and the record of distinctions were furnished by the present corresponding secretaries. Although no distinctions are mentioned except such as are considered important at the several colleges, nevertheless, in accordance with the plan of the book, more distinctions are named than would have place in a catalogue of the whole fraternity.

The notes prefixed to each chapter's roll were prepared by the editor and sent to the chapters for correction. In the paragraphs regarding fraternities in general, chapters are named in the order of original foundation. In the paragraphs regarding our own chapters, the lists of corresponding secretaries, of delegates to convention, and of other officers are, as a matter of course, limited to the period explained above.

Although the whole of the book was prepared and edited by one person, every one knows that a book like this must, in a very important sense, be the work of numerous hands. It is merely a compilation, and for materials it is largely indebted to records kept by corresponding secretaries, general secretaries, secretaries of conventions, and secretaries of the board of directors.

*Eugene Wambaugh.*

Cincinnati, O., April 21, 1886.

# CONTENTS.

# Hand-Book of 1886

---

## NOTES ON THE RECENT HISTORY OF BETA THETA PI.

### THE PURPOSE OF THESE NOTES.

Beginning with the Chicago convention of 1881, these notes come down to the spring of 1886. It must be understood, however, that they do not purport to be a history. A history, if constructed with due attention to perspective, ignores many events and discusses only the most important ; and, besides, a history gives great attention to causes and results. These notes, on the contrary, having no such ambitious design, do not attempt to make a selection of the most important events, and still less do they pretend to give discussions of sources and tendencies. Perhaps the time has not come when a good history of these recent years can be written; but, whether the time has come or not, these notes have a very different purpose. Many of the events of these few years will have no place in a history of the whole life of the fraternity: and yet it is important that at the present and for some time to come our members keep in mind these very events, no matter how unimportant they may, by and by, appear ; for the same matters will probably come up again and again, and, in order that there may be intelligent discussion and action, every one ought to know what has been our recent policy. Of course, a great deal can be learned from the minutes of the conventions; but there are very few complete sets. Besides, the minutes are published in such a shape that it is not always easy to learn at a glance just what was finally done by the conventions, for there is constant reference back and forth to exhibits. Accordingly, it is not improbable that the review here given of the recent conventions and of other events will be a convenience even to the possessors of full sets of minutes. The attempt has been to omit nothing that can conceivably be of interest, and when there has been any doubt as to the importance of matter the decision has been to include rather than to exclude.

### CONVENTION OF 1881.

The forty-second annual convention was held in Chicago on August 30th and 31st and September 1st, 1881. The Grand Pacific Hotel was the headquarters. About two hundred and twenty-five members were present. The business meetings were held in the Appellate Court room, a large and well-appointed apartment in one of the wings of the hotel. Thirty-four college chapters were represented, namely: Beloit, Bethany, Boston, Brown, California, Centre, Cornell, Denison, DePauw, Hampden Sidney, Hanover, Harvard, Indiana, Iowa, Johns Hopkins, Kansas, Kenyon, Madison, Michigan, Northwestern, Ohio, Ohio Wesleyan, Pennsylvania, Richmond, St. Lawrence, Stevens, Virginia, Wabash, Washington and Jefferson, Western Reserve, Westminster, Wisconsin, Wittenberg, Wooster. The only college chapters not represented were Cumberland, Dickinson, Iowa Wesleyan, Maine State, Mississippi, Randolph Macon, Rutgers, Trinity University, and Union. Delegates were present from seven alumni chapters, namely: Baltimore, Chicago, Cincinnati, Cleveland, Indianapolis, Richmond (Va.), and New York.

Hon. Mark L. DeMotte was temporary chairman and W. B. Cady was temporary secretary. The permanent officers were Chief Justice Alonzo P. Carpenter, of New Hampshire, president: E. H. Terrell, Guy C. Earl, Willoughby N. Smith, D. E. Osborne, A. P. Hoyt, Harry F. Ehrman, and C. D. Williams, vice-presidents; W. R. Baird, secretary: W. B. Cady, J. C. Hanna, and E. H. Ernst, assistant secretaries. O. R. Brouse was chairman of the committee on constitution and jurisprudence. E. H. Terrell was chairman of the committee on chapters and charters.

The report of the general secretary, Rev. E. J. Brown, was an able and comprehensive document. a fit conclusion to that conscientious officer's three years of laborious service. It gave a sketch of the fraternity's history for the academic year just ended and an account of the condition and prospects of the several chapters, with a statistical table, which showed that during 1880–81 there had been 256 initiates and a total active membership of 601. A feature of the table was the classifying of each chapter's prospects as "very good," "good," and "fair." The report laid before the convention the petition from Columbia, suggested that legislation be had regarding alumni chapters, and presented a code of laws establishing a general secretary's roll of new members. The report gave. at considerable length, the reasons why three petitions had been sent directly to the chapters, and said that in the future "all petitions for charters should be retained for the consideration of the convention, unless the circumstances of the petition themselves make it plainly exceptional."

The board of directors, by W. F. Boyd, its secretary, presented a report that gave particular prominence to the work done, partly by order of the convention of 1880 and partly of the board's own motion, in investigating the condition of several chapters. Three chapters had been requested by the board, after careful investigation by a special commissioner, to resign their charters, and had done so. This action of the board was unanimously approved by the convention. The report laid before the convention some papers regarding the condition and prospects of Trinity University. One of these papers was a report from the special commissioner appointed by the board to visit that chapter. On account of an emphatic protest from the chapter's alumni the board had decided not to suspend the charter. The papers were laid before the

convention without recommendation. The convention withdrew the charter of the Trinity University chapter. Ohio University and Westminster chapters and Chicago alumni were the only chapters that voted in the negative.

This convention granted formal charters, as required by the constitution, to the chapters that had been established since the last convention. The only new chapter chartered was Columbia. There was a petition from the University of Nebraska which, on account of a defect in the papers, could not be put to a vote. The defect was that the sentiment of the three neighboring chapters had not been formally obtained. The following resolution was adopted: "Resolved, That the petition for a charter at the University of Nebraska, which this convention has not been able to act upon by reason of imperfection of the papers, shall, when put in constitutional shape for action through the general secretary, be immediately put to a vote of the chapters by the board of directors." No one called attention to the fact that this resolution was so worded as to take from the general secretary and the board the constitutional right and duty of determining, after thorough investigation, whether the circumstances of the case are so extraordinary as to warrant the adoption of the short way of treating petitions. The resolution was adopted in order to gratify the petitioners, who had long been waiting patiently, and who were likely to complain of a delay for which they were in no way responsible. Edwin H. Terrell wrote the resolution, and wrote it very hastily. In the carefully-prepared report of the committee on constitution and jurisprudence, written and presented by him as chairman of the committee, occurs the following passage, which had already been adopted by the convention: "As the petition is not recommended by the two of the three nearest chapters to the site of the University of Nebraska, we refer the petition back to the convention as not ready to be acted upon. We recommend that the petition be retained by the general secretary until the proper recommendations have been secured, when it may again be submitted to the fraternity." This latter wording is more careful, and is not open to any constitutional objection. The only objection to it was that it did not contain any suggestion that the petition might be sent around the short way. So far as the recommendation went, the petitioners had no encouragement to hope that their petition would be acted upon before the next convention. When this fact was noticed, Terrell hastily wrote the resolution given above. It is unfortunate that he did not copy the words of the recommendation which, as chairman of the committee on chapters and charters, he had made regarding another petition, namely, "That it be referred to the board of directors and general secretary for further investigation, to be submitted by them to a vote of the chapters as soon as possible under the emergency clause, if by them deemed advisable." This last is a very accurate piece of wording. Yet the loose and inaccurate wording of the hastily-drawn resolution has served as the model for subsequent recommendations; and in consequence one of the most careful of our fraternity jurists has become innocently responsible for a blunder that may, by and by, cause serious disagreement as to the right of a convention to limit the powers that by the constitution are given to the other branches of the government.

Before the Chicago convention the legislative acts other than the constitution itself had been called by-laws. The convention changed this name to laws, principally for the reason that by-laws is a term more appropriately given to the regulations of a chapter. The convention made no material changes in the laws already existing, but made several valuable additions. It adopted the general secretary's suggestion regarding a roll of new members. The difficulty of preparing the catalogue of 1881 had suggested the advisability of keeping a roll upon which should be entered the name of each new member. The legislation adopted at Chicago on this subject has been very useful, and has not been altered.

Six sections were adopted with reference to alumni chapters, being the first legislation on that subject since the adoption of the present constitution. These sections have since been changed in many points, but they are still, in most of the important matters, the basis of the whole law on alumni chapters.

The first law upon dispensations was also adopted. As it is still in force, it may be important to know what were the reasons for its passage. It is sometimes assumed that the law as to dispensa-

tions gives to a chapter, with permission of the board, the power to initiate men who, in the absence of this law, would not be eligible. That is an error. So far as the constitution goes, any chapter may elect and initiate a student of any college whatever, and, provided the candidate be a student of some college. it is not necessary that he be a student of the college where the chapter is situated. The right to initiate students of other colleges had seldom or never been exercised by any chapter, but there were reports that the right had been exercised, and, therefore, the convention, wishing to place some restriction upon such initiations, passed the law forbidding a chapter to "elect or initiate any person not a student in some department of the institution in which the chapter is located." except "that in cases of obvious expediency the board of directors may grant a dispensation allowing the initiation of students in other institutions."

The convention placed on record and recommended to the chapters the official seal used in 1839. It is still the official seal of chapters.

Three sections were adopted with reference to jurisdiction, procedure, and penalties in cases of discipline.

As these various additions to the laws were very important, and as the laws were now numerous and scattered, the board of directors and the general secretary were directed to collect all of the laws and to arrange and publish them in the form of a code.

Besides making these important additions to the laws, the convention took action on many other matters of permanent interest. It instructed the directors to "take such measures as may to them seem most advisable to secure the co-operation of the leading college fraternities in a movement to discourage and abolish the practice of making combinations for the purpose of affecting elections to college offices and honors." Unfortunately, this early movement in the direction of pan-hellenism came to nothing. Other votes that had little or no practical result were that the directors should enroll in a book the proceedings of all conventions since the organization of the fraternity and the proceedings of all future conventions; that there should be a standing committee on alumni chapters to encourage and stimulate the organizing of such chapters and to report to the next convention; that there should be a similar standing committee on chapter houses; and that William R. Baird be editor of a manual which should contain constitution, laws, record of conventions, lists of chapters, statistics, lists of prominent men, a short sketch of fraternity history, lists of rivals, and official documents.

The convention voted that each jeweler to the fraternity must pay an annual royalty of fifty dollars. This is still the rule.

This convention attempted to settle the question regarding initiating preparatory students. The Baltimore convention of 1880, by a vote of 66 to 12, had resolved "That this convention emphatically reaffirms the requirements of our constitution permitting the initiation of members of undergraduate classes only, and demands that the chapters entirely abandon the practice of initiating preparatory students or other ineligible persons." It will be noticed that that resolution was not, in form, at least, an attempt to legislate under the pretense of interpreting already existing law. The Baltimore doctrine was brought up at the Chicago convention. The committee on constitution and jurisprudence reported a resolution that "The sense of the convention is that the initiation of preparatory students be in every way discouraged." That mild resolution did not suit the convention, and instead it was, by a vote of 28 to 5, resolved "That, in institutions having a preparatory department attached as a part of their collegiate system, the classes in which are under charge of and taught by the college professors, and are carried on the college catalogue, such preparatory department may be construed as coming within the constitutional designation of undergraduate classes, until otherwise ordered by a general convention of the fraternity." As this resolution was disapproved by the next convention, there is no need of discussing what effect, if any, this legislative interpretation had upon the constitution.

There was universal regret that Rev. E. J. Brown, general secretary, and C. J. Seaman, song-book agent, refused to retain the offices that they had so long filled. The officers elected for the ensuing year were Eugene Wambaugh, general secretary; J. S. Goodwin and E. J. Brown, historiographers; Major W. C. Ransom, visiting officer; C. J. Seaman, catalogue agent; W. H. January, song-

book agent; Dr. Thad. A. Reamy, W. F. Boyd, and O. R. Brouse, directors for three years.

The literary exercises were held in Fairbank Hall, on the evening of August 30th. The orator was Rev. John Bascom, president of the University of Wisconsin. The poet was the Hon. W. F. Stone, one of the justices of the supreme court of Colorado. The banquet was had in the Grand Pacific Hotel on the evening of the 31st. Gen. R. W. Smith presided. Responses were made by Hon. Mark L. DeMotte, Dr. Theophilus Parvin, Col. C. C. Matson, Hon. Schuyler Colfax, Hon. A. P. Carpenter, Hon. John W. Herron, and Rev. J. Hogarth Lozier. Some of the music was furnished by the Beta Theta Pi quartette from the University of Michigan. Three hundred gentlemen and ladies were present. In every respect the banquet was the most successful ever enjoyed by the fraternity.

The Chicago convention is to this day regarded by every one as the ideal convention. At some conventions there have been as many chapters represented, and at some the social features have been just as pleasant, but, taking everything into the account, the convention of 1881 still stands at the head.

### 1881–'82.

During the year 1881–'82 the board of directors was constituted as follows: Hon. John W. Herron, president; W. F. Boyd, secretary; John I. Covington, R. Harvey Young, Sylvester G. Williams, Dr. Thad. A. Reamy, Major W. C. Ransom, Dr. W. P. Watson, and O. R. Brouse. The board elected R. Harvey Young general treasurer, John I. Covington editor of the magazine, and S. G. Williams, Willis O. Robb, and William R. Baird assistants.

The board confirmed the general secretary's new division of the fraternity into districts and his appointment of chief assistant secretaries as follows: I., New England, John T. Blodgett; II., New York and New Jersey, W. R. Baird; III., Pennsylvania, Delaware, Maryland, District of Columbia, and West Virginia, Willoughby N. Smith; IV., Virginia, North Carolina, and South Carolina, Jas. G. Field, Jr.; V., Kentucky, Tennessee, Georgia, Florida, Alabama, Mississippi, and Louisiana, John A. Heron; VI., Ohio, Chas. H. Carey; VII.,

Indiana and Michigan, A. N. Grant; VIII., Illinois, Wisconsin, Minnesota, and Iowa, W. A. Hamilton; IX., the other states and territories, Scott Hopkins.

The number of chapters remained the same as the previous year—forty-three, Columbia taking the place of Trinity University. The Columbia chapter was established on October 28th, 1881, by Harvey F. Mitchell, special commissioner. The petition from the University of Nebraska was sent around in the short way by the general secretary and the board, as ordered by the convention. It was rejected. Petitions from Illinois Industrial University and Mercer University failed to obtain the approval of the neighboring chapters. Petitions from Pennsylvania College and several other institutions were discouraged, the very slightest investigation showing that it would be a waste of time to entertain them for an instant. A petition from Vanderbilt University was deemed by the board to be worthy of attention. The general secretary was instructed to visit the university and report the facts. The result was that, after meeting the petitioners, the chancellor of the university, and others, the general secretary reported that, although the petitioners were excellent men, legislation hostile to fraternities made it inexpedient to grant the charter. At this time the general secretary visited the Cumberland chapter, which had been for a year or two inactive and almost dead. Upon receiving the general secretary's report regarding Vanderbilt and Cumberland, the board granted a dispensation allowing the Cumberland chapter to elect and initiate Vanderbilt students. The purpose was to strengthen Cumberland and to retain our influence at Vanderbilt. Both purposes were admirably served by this dispensation. It should be known that this dispensation, like all others, was limited as to time, and was renewed from year to year.

The laws adopted by the convention of 1881 compelled the alumni chapters to reorganize. Baltimore, Chicago, Cincinnati, Cleveland, Indianapolis, and Richmond (Va.) did so. There were also large re-unions at Providence, Indianapolis, and Kansas City.

The chief event of the year was the publication of the catalogue of 1881. This was given to subscribers in December.

It was a vast advance upon our previous catalogues. The difficulties of the work performed by the editor, Chas. J. Seaman, and his two associates, William R. Baird and Edwin H. Terrell, can never be fully appreciated. Their catalogue was our first attempt in the line of modern biographical cataloguing, and will be of incalculable assistance to all future editors.

The magazine was even better than in previous years. It added to the old features a series of articles descriptive of various American colleges. The piece of work for which this volume of the magazine will be longest remembered is the suggestion of a pan-hellenic council. This suggestion originated with our fraternity, and Willis O. Robb is the person to whom the honor belongs.

### CONVENTION OF 1882.

The sessions of the forty-third annual convention were held at Cincinnati on August 29th, 30th, and 31st, 1882. The sessions of the first day were held at Melodeon Hall. The subsequent ones were held in the law school of the Cincinnati College. The convention had headquarters at the Gibson House. One hundred and eighty-five members were present. Thirty-one college chapters were represented, namely, Boston, Brown, Centre, Cornell, Denison, DePauw, Hampden Sidney, Hanover, Harvard, Indiana, Iowa, Kenyon, Madison, Maine State, Michigan, Mississippi, Northwestern, Ohio, Ohio Wesleyan, Randolph Macon, Richmond, St. Lawrence, Stevens, Union, Virginia, Wabash, Western Reserve, Westminster, Wisconsin, Wittenberg, and Wooster. The college chapters not represented were Beloit, Bethany, California, Columbia, Cumberland, Dickinson, Iowa Wesleyan, Johns Hopkins, Kansas, Pennsylvania, Rutgers, and Washington and Jefferson. Chicago, Cincinnati, Cleveland, and Indianapolis alumni chapters were represented.

The temporary officers were O. R. Brouse, chairman, and J. R. Moorehead, secretary. The permanent officers were Hon. Will Cumback, president; H. S. Babcock, W. E. Jobbins, H. S. Steller, F. B. Clark, A. C. Downs, J. C. Hanna, J. E. Beal, W. A. Hamilton, and J. Wallace Childs, vice-presidents; F. W. Shepardson, secretary; J. A. Case and Wm. Iglehart, assistant secretaries. Gen. R. W. Smith was chairman of the committee on constitution and jurisprudence; and Rev. E. J. Brown was chairman of the committee on chapters and charters.

The general secretary's report detailed the year's history, named three chapters that were so weak as to need investigation, presented petitions from Colby University and Vanderbilt University, submitted a code that he had compiled in pursuance of the action of the convention of 1881, and discussed several questions that had arisen in managing the roll. The report was accompanied by a map of the fraternity and by a table of statistics, which, besides giving the usual figures as to membership and initiations, classified our active members by classes and courses and gave some figures regarding our rivals and regarding non-fraternity men.

The figures for 1881-'82 were as follows : 43 chapters ; 586 active members : by classes, 134 seniors, 116 juniors, 136 sophomores, 129 freshmen, 27 preparatory students, 44 post-graduate and professional ; by courses, 340 classical, 155 scientific, philosophical, and literary, 50 technological, 11 medical, 23 law, 7 post-graduates ; 209 initiates. These figures are taken from the statistical table, which was like all those since prepared, except that it attempted to give some indication of college honors taken by our members and also to give the relative standing of our rivals at the various colleges.

Letters of regret were read from numerous distinguished men. A letter was read from the University of California chapter, approving the petitions for charters. This was spread upon the minutes. A letter from Major Ransom was read and spread upon the minutes, giving the convention fatherly advice upon several subjects and especially opposing the granting of one of the petitions for a charter.

The Colby petition was rejected. The general secretary was ordered to submit the Vanderbilt petition to the chapters within two months after the convention. The three weak chapters mentioned in the general secretary's report were admonished that they must improve before the meeting of the next convention.

The code, or compilation of laws edited by the general secretary, was approved. The constitution and laws were amended so as to provide for a convention assessment fund. This was, of course, subject to approval by the next convention, as constitutional amendments must be approved by two conventions. A constitutional amendment making conventions biennial was also passed, subject to approval by the next convention ; but the convention was really not in favor of the amendment, and adopted it only to please Gen. R. W. Smith and to give him an opportunity to have the amendment discussed for a year and to have it finally acted upon in 1882. The cases arising in the general secretary's management of the roll were disposed of by censuring the chapters that had been guilty of irregularities in initiating ineligible persons. The resolution of the convention of 1881 as to the initiation of preparatory students was repealed by a vote of 33 to 6 ; and regarding this subject no other action was taken. The convention had the advantage of having before it an elaborate report upon this question, prepared by W. A. Hamilton at the request of the board of directors. The general secretary was instructed to publish his code, embodying in it the laws as amended by the convention. This was done immediately, the code being published as part of the minutes.

Willis O. Robb, Eugene Wambaugh, and John T. Blodgett were appointed to confer with other fraternities with reference to a pan-hellenic council. A committee was appointed to revise the ritual and report to the next convention, and it was ordered that until the new ritual was adopted the chapters should confine themselves to the ritual adopted by the Baltimore convention or by previous conventions. As the new ritual has never been prepared, this last order is the law to this day. It was voted that William R. Baird be editor of the manual, with Ransom, Seaman, Babcock, Brouse, Robb, and Terrell as an advisory and revisionary committee. It was also ordered that the history prepared by John S. Goodwin be by him revised and completed, under the supervision of the board, and be then bound in substantial form and filed in the archives.

The following officers were elected for the ensuing year : Eugene Wambaugh, general secretary ; John S. Goodwin and Rev. E. J. Brown, historiographers ; Chas. J. Seaman, catalogue agent ; W. H. January, song-book agent ; Major W. C. Ransom, visiting officer ; Hon. John W. Herron, John I. Covington, and Major W. C. Ransom, directors for three years. The literary exercises were held at

Melodeon Hall, on the evening of August 29th. Gov. A. G. Porter, of Indiana, was the orator, and H. S. Babcock was the poet. Remarks were made by Hon. Will Cumback and by Hon. John Reily Knox, one of the founders of the fraternity. This convention had more than an average share of attention from our older members. During the regular sessions speeches were made by Gen. Durbin Ward. Governor T. T. Crittenden, of Missouri, and Dr. Ormond Beatty, president of Centre College. At the banquet responses were made by Hon. Will Cumback, Rev. L. G. Hay, Gen. R. W. Smith, Dr. E. E. Edwards, and D. G. Hamilton (reading a response written by Hon. Sidney Thomas, who was detained by sickness). A poem was read by H. S. Babcock. Dr. Thad. A. Reamy was the toast-master. A novel feature was the presence of a member of another fraternity, Hon. S. F. Hunt, who responded to the sentiment "The Pan-hellenic Council." This banquet was held at the Gibson House on the evening of August 31st. About two hundred gentlemen and ladies were present. Like the Chicago banquet, it was given at the expense of local alumni. It is probable that the great expense of these two banquets suggested the change since adopted, whereby the alumni are relieved from this burden.

### 1882-'83.

During the year 1882-'83 the board of directors was constituted precisely as in the preceding year, except that Sylvester G. Williams became the secretary. The editors of the magazine were Willis O. Robb, Chas. M. Hepburn, W. C. Sprague, and W. R. Baird. The business managers were Frank M. Joyce and E. W. Runyan.

The division into districts remained as in the preceding year, except that West Virginia was transferred from District III. to District IV. The chief assistant secretaries for the districts were I., John T. Blodgett ; II., E. D. W. Petteys ; III., Willoughby N. Smith; IV., W. C. White; V., A. C. Downs ; VI., J. C. Hanna ; VII., A. N. Grant ; VIII., W. A. Hamilton ; IX., Scott Hopkins.

No new chapters were established. The Vanderbilt petitioners decided to wait another year, hoping that meanwhile the anti-fraternity law would be repealed. The dispensation allowing Cumberland chapter to initiate Vanderbilt students was continued. Petitions from Syracuse University, Colby University, and Ohio State University failed to obtain the approval of the neighboring chapters. A dispensation was granted to Ohio Wesleyan chapter allowing the initiation of the Ohio State University petitioners. The reason for this action was that the neighboring chapters joined in a request that there be this recognition of the persistent loyalty shown by the petitioners during the several years spent in fruitlessly working for a charter. Alumni chapters were established in Providence and New York. There were large reunions at Indianapolis and Providence.

The magazine more that sustained the reputation of former years. The editorial articles were more elaborate than before, and had an excellent literary finish. The items regarding other fraternities were numerous. In fact, there was an improvement in every respect. The reason for the improvement was that there was a larger board of editors than before ; and, besides, the editors were relieved of the business management.

This year was marked by an advance in the character of the magazines of most of the fraternities. The fraternity magazines were more numerous, better, and more liberal in exchanging with one another. This may have been a result of the general discussion of a pan-hellenic council. In accordance with a call issued by the editors of the BETA THETA PI, a preliminary meeting of representatives of various fraternities was held at Philadelphia on the 22d of February, 1882, Willis O. Robb, the first advocate of the movement, representing us by appointment of the last convention. This meeting made arrangements for a pan-hellenic council to be held in 1884. Several subjects for discussion were announced. Nothing ever resulted from these arrangements, except that since 1882 willingness to co-operate and kindly feeling towards one another have been much more noticeable than before.

In May, 1882, the general secretary visited the chapters at Dickinson, Johns Hopkins, the University of Pennsylvania, Rutgers, Stevens, Columbia, Brown, Boston, Harvard, Maine State, Union, Madison, Cornell, and St. Lawrence. Besides visiting these fourteen chapters, he met the Colby petitioners and visited Amherst. As the Amherst petition had not yet been actually signed, his presence at Amherst was kept a secret from the petitioners, and it is probable that our Amherst members now learn for the first time that they were carefully examined by the general secretary before their case was acted upon by the fraternity. It was necessary to make this investigation of Amherst thus early and secretly, because the petition was not to be signed until the undergraduate and alumni petitioners met at commencement, and, of course, a thorough examination could not be made between commencement and the convention. As every crowd of petitioners ought to be examined by an officer of the fraternity, the examination in this case had to be made before the petition was signed, unless the whole matter was to be postponed for one year. Care was taken, however, that the prospective petitioners should know nothing of the general secretary's presence, lest they should suppose that he had actually come all the way from Cincinnati to attempt to influence them.

### CONVENTION OF 1883.

The forty-fourth annual convention met at Saratoga Springs on August 28th, 29th, and 30th, 1883, with headquarters at Congress Hall. About eighty members were present. Twenty-three college chapters were represented, namely, Boston, Brown, Centre, Columbia, Cornell, Denison, DePauw, Harvard, Indiana, Kansas, Kenyon, Madison, Maine State, Michigan, Northwestern, Ohio Wesleyan, Pennsylvania, St. Lawrence, Stevens, Union, Virginia, Western Reserve, Wooster. Therefore the college chapters not represented were Beloit, Bethany, California, Cumberland, Dickinson, Hampden Sidney, Hanover, Iowa, Iowa Wesleyan, Johns Hopkins, Mississippi, Ohio, Randolph Macon, Richmond, Rutgers, Wabash, Washington and Jefferson, Westminster, Wisconsin, and Wittenberg. The alumni chapters at Chicago, Cincinnati, Cleveland, New York, Providence, and Richmond, Va., sent delegates.

The opening session was held at the hotel, but all of the other sessions were held at the City Hall, in the room of the supreme court. Willis O. Robb was the temporary chairman and Richard Lee Fearn was the temporary secretary. The permanent officers were Major W. C. Ransom, president ; Chas. J. Seaman, S. G. Williams, and A. H. Flack, vice-presidents ; F. C. McMillan, secretary ; A. M. Dyer and R. L. Fearn, assistant secretaries. J. E. Heath was chairman of the committee on constitution and jurisprudence, and J. C. Bannister was chairman of the committee on chapters and charters.

The table of statistics presented with the general secretary's report showed for 1882-'83, 43 college chapters, with a membership of 586 ; by classes, 114 seniors, 122 juniors, 142 sophomores, 136 freshmen, 14 preparatory, 58 post-graduate and professional ; by courses, 330 studying for A. B., 148 S. B., Ph. B., and Lit. B., 51 C. E. Agr., B., or other technological degrees, 10 M. D., 34 LL. B., 3 S. T. B., 10 post-graduate ; 229 initiates.

The general secretary's report gave a review of the year's work and presented petitions from Vanderbilt, Emory, and Amherst. The Amherst petition was granted. The other two were refused.

Several constitutional amendments were acted upon. The amendment substituting biennial conventions for annual conventions came up for final action and was not adopted. The amendment creating the convention assessment fund was adopted, and, having been approved by the preceding convention, became part of the constitution. An amendment providing that conventions shall meet at Cincinnati not once in three years but once in four years received the approval of this convention and was referred to the next for final action. An important amendment making possible a change in the system of naming college chapters was also approved, subject to the action of the next convention, and the general secretary was instructed to prepare a system and submit it with his next annual report.

To avoid all questions as to the force of laws not contained in the code, all laws passed previously to the adoption of the code were repealed. This convention made very insignificant additions to the laws, as distinguished from the constitution. It was enacted that the total annual assessment for annual dues upon each alumni chapter should be $12 ; that the board should send an annual letter to the alumni of dead chapters ; and that alumni not members of alumni chapters should pay an annual assessment of one dollar. These laws, like the laws of 1882 creating the convention assessment fund, have not been enforced.

Willis O. Robb, who had represented us at the preliminary pan-hellenic conference, presented a report of the actions of that body. The convention appointed delegates to represent us at the expected council. A committee was, as usual, appointed to gather ideas as to alumni chapters and report to the next convention. It was also voted that the subscription price of the magazine ought to be $2 : but, as every one knows, this recommendation has never been followed.

The officers elected for the ensuing year were R. Harvey Young, William B. Burnet, and Hon. Peleg Emory Aldrich, directors for three years ; Eugene Wambaugh, general secretary ; Chas. J. Seaman, catalogue agent ; W. H. January, song-book agent ; John S. Goodwin, historiographer ; and L. C. Hascall, visiting officer.

At the public exercises the oration was delivered by Dr. C. N. Sims, chancellor of Syracuse University. The banquet was the first one given on the modern plan of finances, each man paying for his ticket. Owing to the very small number of local alumni the attendance was not as large as at most banquets. Willis O. Robb was master of ceremonies. Addresses were made by Major W. C. Ransom, John Reily Knox, A. A. Alling, Gen. Gates P. Thruston, and Sylvester G. Williams.

This convention, being held at a great summer resort, was tempted to give comparatively little attention to business. It managed, however, to attend to business well, and to enjoy itself also. The convention in a body enjoyed a coach ride to the park and to Saratoga Lake, and made an expedition to Mt. McGregor. After the convention closed, many of the delegates went upon an excursion to Lake George and elsewhere. Indeed, the features of a pleasure trip were noticeable even before the convention began : for on the way to Saratoga a large party of delegates met at Chautauqua Lake, and then and there formed the scheme of the Beta Theta Pi alumni club-house at Wooglin. Thus it happened that the Saratoga convention, though one of the smallest, is one of the most memorable. It is also memorable as probably the only convention that has been successfully photographed.

### 1883-'84.

During 1883-'84 the districts remained as in the preceding year. A slight change was made in the method of selecting the chiefs. Formerly men of considerable age and experience, generally alumni, were selected. This year the method was changed, and choice was made of men who in the preceding year had been efficient corresponding secretaries. Thus it happened that several of the new chiefs were undergraduates. This change was made in order to call attention to the importance of the corresponding secretary's office and in order to reward those who performed the duties of that office with promptness and good judgment. This principle of selecting chiefs is still followed. The chiefs of districts for the year were : I., W. M. McInnes ; II., F. Dixon Hall ; III., Howard S. Stetler ; IV., Norborne R. Clarke ; V., Chas. L. Jungerman ; VI., James A. Robbach ; VII., James Albert Case ; VIII., H. P. Mozier ; IX., Chas. S. Wheeler.

The board of directors was constituted as follows : Hon. John W. Herron, president ; W. B. Burnet, secretary ; Dr. Thad. A. Reamy, W. F. Boyd, John I. Covington, R. Harvey Young, O. R. Brouse, Major W. C. Ransom, and Hon. Peleg Emory Aldrich. R. Harvey Young was general treasurer. Chambers Baird, Jr., was managing editor of the magazine and Chas. M. Hepburn, William R. Baird, and F. W. Shepardson were his associates. The business management was in the hands of F. M. Joyce, M. P. Drury, E. L. Martin, and S. S. Kauffmann. The magazine was changed to the present form. Nine numbers were published, making a total of four hundred and thirty-two pages. When the size of the page and the style of the typography are taken into the account, it appears that the magazine gave more matter than has ever been given by our magazine or by any similar one. It is more important to notice that the magazine was also better than ever before. The editorial department maintained the standard of previous years, and the improved typography seemed to raise the standard of the other departments. However that may be, it is a fact that this volume saw a vast improvement in chapter letters and in personal items. An interesting feature was a series of "Fraternity Studies" by Wm. R. Baird. There were also several valuable articles upon subjects not connected with fraternity work. This last was an experiment in the direction of combining the functions

of a literary magazine with those of a
fraternity organ, after the fashion proposed
by Beta Theta Pi more than forty years
ago. The experiment can never be more
skillfully tried than it was in 1883–84, and
no one could wish a greater literary
success than the magazine was in that
year ; but it appeared to be a fact that
the subscribers to this magazine subscribe
for it in order to obtain matter regarding
our fraternity, other fraternities, and similar subjects, and prefer to get their general
literature elsewhere. Therefore, the semi-
literary plan has been abandoned, and
the ambition of subsequent editors has
been the ambition of the earlier ones,
namely, to, make a magazine that will
give fraternity news and discuss fraternity
subjects in a style that will not offend
good taste.

The Amherst chapter was established
October 12th, 1883. W. M. McInnes was
the commissioner. The Vanderbilt petition was also finally granted. The Vanderbilt anti-fraternity laws were repealed
in November, 1883, and as soon there-
after as possible the petition was submitted to the chapters in the short way.
The chapter was formally established on
February 23d, 1884. Gen. Gates P.
Thruston being the chairman of the com-
mission appointed to take charge of the
ceremony. From the adjournment of the
Chicago convention in 1881 to the meeting of the St. Louis convention in 1883,
Amherst and Vanderbilt were the only
charters granted. There was an analogy
between the two cases. Each chapter was
established after the petitioners had had
prolonged experience in fraternity matters. The Amherst petitioners had for five
years been a local society called the Torch
and Crown, and had demonstrated their
ability to succeed in the face of the oldest
fraternities. Many of the Vanderbilt men
had for two years been members of our
fraternity, initiated at Cumberland under
dispensations ; and they had been main-
taining something like a chapter organization. They were strong and had shown
that even when opposed by anti-fraternity
laws it was easy, for them to get excellent
men. Neither at Amherst nor at Vanderbilt did we run any risk of finding that
our petitioners did not know how to
manage a fraternity. Another similarity
between the two institutions was that
each was in the first rank.

Alumni chapters were established at
Boston and Wheeling. Minor matters

were petitions from Syracuse University,
Central University, the University of
Georgia, and the Southwestern Presbyterian University. None of these obtained
the approval of the neighboring chapters.
In 1884 the new song-book was published by the song-book agent. W. H.
January. It was larger than the previous
collections, and contained the music scores
in full.

The most memorable event of the year
was the perfecting of the club-house
scheme. Enough stock was taken to
make the scheme a success, the ground
was bought, and the association was incorporated in Ohio as the Beta Theta Pi
Alumni Club, with headquarters at Cleveland. Most of the credit is due to Chas.
J. Seaman, who was enthusiastically
seconded by Edwin H. Terrell and W.
K. L. Warwick. In the spring the club-
house was built on the club's grounds, at
Wooglin on Chautauqua Lake. The place
for holding the convention of 1884 was
Cleveland ; but the board of directors, at
the request of all concerned, changed the
place to Wooglin.

CONVENTION OF 1884.

The forty-fifth annual convention was
the first one held in a building belonging to the fraternity. The convention
met in the Beta Theta Pi alumni club-
house, at Wooglin, on Chautauqua Lake,
New York, on August 19th, 20th, 21st,
and 22d, 1884. About one hundred members were present. Thirty-seven college
chapters were represented, namely, Amherst, Bethany, Boston, Brown, California,
Centre, Columbia, Cornell, Denison, De
Pauw, Hampden Sidney, Harvard, Indiana, Iowa, Johns Hopkins, Kansas,
Kenyon, Madison, Maine State, Michigan,
Northwestern, Ohio, Ohio Wesleyan,
Pennsylvania, Randolph Macon, St. Lawrence, Stevens, Union, Vanderbilt, Virginia, Wabash, Washington and Jefferson,
Western Reserve, Westminster, Wisconsin, Wittenberg, and Wooster. Seven
college chapters were not represented,
namely, Beloit, Cumberland, Dickinson,
Hanover, Iowa Wesleyan, Mississippi,
Richmond, and Rutgers. The alumni
chapters at Chicago, Cincinnati, Cleveland, Providence, and Wheeling were
represented. Thus, although this was not
a large convention, the number of college
chapters represented was larger than ever
before.

Chas. L. Jungerman was temporary chairman and T. C. Elliott was temporary secretary. The permanent organization was as follows : Edwin H. Terrell, president ; Charles S. Wheeler, Thomas D. Wood, and Chambers Baird, Jr., vice-presidents ; Jacob Brilles, secretary ; J. J. G. Ruhn and R. B. Bloodgood, assistant secretaries. A. P. Sumner was chairman of the committee on constitution and jurisprudence. Chambers Baird, Jr., was chairman of the committee on chapters and charters.

The general secretary's report suggested that in order to provide for better performance of the numerous duties of his department there should be added a college secretary and an alumni secretary : called attention to the fact that an important part of the question of extension is the necessity of having an administrative system capable of managing from fifty to a hundred chapters ; presented petitions from the University of Minnesota, the Ohio State University, and Denver University ; and laid before the convention, as required by the previous convention, the best system that he could devise for naming the college chapters. His tabular view of statistics showed for 1883-'84 forty-five college chapters, with total membership of 624 ; by classes, 117 seniors, 124 juniors, 147 sophomores, 153 freshmen, 24 preparatory, 59 professional and post-graduates ; by courses, 354 for A. B., 147 for S. B., Ph. B., or Lit. B., 62 for C. E., Agr. B., and other technological degrees, 13 for M. D., 27 for LL. B., 6 for S. T. B., and 14 post-graduates ; 273 initiates.

The report of the board of directors said that as some members of the fraternity seemed to object to the granting of dispensations, the board had decided to grant no more unless the convention should take some action upon the subject. The convention declared its approval of the system of granting dispensations in all cases deemed by the board to be extraordinary. It rejected all of the petitions for charters. Motions were made to withdraw the charters of four chapters, but these motions were voted down. The final action upon this subject was that the board was instructed to make an investigation of the condition of three certain chapters ; and, if it seemed desirable to withdraw the charters, the board was empowered to request a surrender of the same.

It was voted that in case any chapter was not represented by a duly accredited delegate, any member of the chapter would be recognized as a representative. This was a formal recognition of the practice that has for many years obtained. The convention adopted finally the amendment to the constitution regarding names of chapters, and adopted finally the admendment making conventions at Cincinnati quadrennial. It also adopted the general secretary's scheme of naming chapters, whereby the full name is in the following form, "the Miami chapter, the Alpha of Beta Theta Pi." All of the general secretary's recommendations regarding names were embodied in the laws as they now stand.

In accordance with a recommendation contained in the report of the board of directors, it was resolved that an act should be prepared providing for a tribunal for the trial of all charges preferred against a member, wherein the penalty of suspension or expulsion is involved. No such bill was presented ; but the convention improved the ancient practice by adopting a series of laws regulating procedure. The standing committee on alumni chapters, appointed at Saratoga, made a report through Major Ransom. The report presented " a code of standard by-laws to the provisions of which all alumni chapters must hereafter conform." The report was adopted.

The following officers were elected : Dr. Thad. A. Reamy, John Reily Knox, and W. F. Boyd, directors for three years ; J. Cal Hanna, general secretary. The catalogue agent, song-book agent, historiographer, and visiting officers were re-elected. R. Harvey Young resigned his membership in the board of directors. This resignation was a great loss to the fraternity, for, as member of the board and as general treasurer, Young had for many years been one of our most valuable officers. Willis O. Robb was elected to fill the remaining two years of Young's unexpired term in the board of directors. The banquet was held at the Grand Hotel, Point Chautauqua. There were no public exercises. The excursions upon the lake and to Niagara were a sufficient relaxation from the work of the convention.

### 1884-'85.

In 1884-85 the general secretary selected as his co-workers Frank B. Pearson for college secretary and Major W. C. Ransom for alumni secretary. By this division of work, rendered possible by the action of the Wooglin convention, the general secretary's department was much strengthened. The districts remained as before, and the following chiefs were appointed : I., T. C. Elliott ; II., Arthur E. Forbes ; III., Frank T. Baker ; IV., H. C. V. Campbell ; V., Charles L. Jungerman : VI., G. P. Thorpe ; VII., John W. Robbins ; VIII., L. P. Conover ; IX., James R Moorehead. The organization of the board of directors was as follows : Hon. John W. Herron, president : Willis O. Robb, secretary ; John I. Covington, Wm. B. Burnet, Dr. Thad. A. Reamy, W. F. Boyd, Major W. C. Ransom, Hon. Peleg Emory Aldrich, John Reily Knox. The general treasurer was John I. Covington.

The managing editor of the magazine was Willis O. Robb. Chambers Baird. Jr., William R. Baird, and F. W. Shepardson were his associates. Frank M. Joyce was the business manager. The financial success of the magazine during the last few years is due to his systematic work and untiring energy. Six numbers were published, the magazine becoming a bi-monthly. The literary tone of previous years was maintained and improved, although the magazine was, in general, restricted to fraternity matter. The chief feature of the volume was the publication of two short stories, "Grif's Candidate " and " His Second Degree." Yet it is more accurate to say that the chief feature of this volume, as well as of the preceding one, was the excellent and even taste shown throughout every department. In those two years when the dragon, the owl, and the dog appeared upon the cover, the magazine attained as high a degree of excellence and of usefulness as it need ever expect or wish, and the aim of the future editors can only be to copy the tone of those two volumes. Alumni chapters were established at Washington, Philadelphia, and Denver. A dispensation was granted to Northwestern chapter, permitting the initiation of students of the University of Denver ; and a dispensation was granted to Hampden Sidney chapter, allowing the initiation of students of the Hampden Sidney Theological Seminary. No new college chapters were established.

### CONVENTION OF 1885.

The sessions of the forty-sixth annual convention were held at the Lindell Hotel, St. Louis, on August 26th, 27th, and 28th, 1885. About sixty members were present, representing the following twenty-two college chapters: Beloit, Bethany, Brown, Centre, Cornell, DePauw, Harvard, Iowa, Iowa Wesleyan, Johns Hopkins, Kansas, Michigan, Mississippi, Ohio, Ohio Wesleyan, Richmond, St. Lawrence, Stevens, Virginia, Westminster, Wisconsin, and Wooster. Twenty-three college chapters were not represented, namely : Amherst, Boston, California, Columbia, Cumberland, Denison, Dickinson, Hampden Sidney, Hanover, Indiana, Kenyon, Madison, Maine State, Northwestern, Pennsylvania, Randolph Macon, Rutgers, Union, Vanderbilt, Wabash, Washington and Jefferson, Western Reserve, and Wittenberg. Several alumni chapters were represented, but it was decided by the chair that alumni chapters which had not since the Wooglin convention reorganized and formally adopted the standard code of by-laws could not be recognized. As there were very few alumni present, this ruling was not tested, and the question will undoubtedly come up for final decision hereafter.

W. W. Dedrick was temporary chairman and C. A. Hall was temporary secretary. The permanent officers were Gov. B. Gratz Brown, president ; Major W. C. Ransom, J. C. Hanna, and Dabney Marshall, vice-presidents ; W. T. Smith, secretary ; C. A. Hall and B. H. Charles, Jr., assistant secretaries. Chambers Baird, Jr., was chairman of the committee on constitution and jurisprudence, and Willis O. Robb was chairman of the committee on chapters and charters.

The board of directors reported a roll of the official names of chapters according to the laws adopted at the Wooglin convention, and reported that there had been a marked improvement in the three chapters whose condition the last convention had instructed the board to investigate. The general secretary reported a prosperous year, presented five petitions for charters, and gave an argument against an extreme conservatism in granting petitions. His table of statistics showed for 1884-'85 forty-five chapters, with a total active membership of 687 ; by classes, 127 seniors, 146 juniors, 162 sophomores, 157 freshmen, 24 preparatory, 67 professional and post-graduate, and 10 unclassified ; by courses, 353 for A. B., 175 for S. B.,

Ph. B., and Lit. B., 61 for C. E., Agr. B., and similar degrees, 15 in special courses, 11 for M. D., 35 for LL. B., 15 for S. T. B., and 18 post-graduates : 248 initiates. A charter was granted to the University of Texas. The other four petitions, including one from the Ohio State University, were ordered to be sent to the chapters by the general secretary in the short way.

It was voted that members of chapters not represented by duly qualified delegates should be allowed to cast the votes of such chapters. It was ruled by the chair that " when the delegation of any chapter consisted of but two members and these two members were divided on any question requiring a vote by chapters, the vote of such a chapter should be considered as cast against the motion before the convention." The vote as to representation of college chapters, the ruling as to divided votes, and the ruling as to alumni chapters are important contributions to our customary law.

The convention did not consider any amendments to the constitution ; and it made no change in the laws, except that it was voted that a chapter transportation fund be formed annually by an assessment of ten dollars upon each active chapter, and that each active chapter must send to convention at least one delegate, whose railroad fare will be paid out of the general transportation fund. The convention authorized that "a clause be placed in the by-laws of every chapter, requiring every active member of the chapter to subscribe to the BETA THETA PI."

It was resolved that "the board of directors be instructed to take into consideration the subject of the semi-centennial anniversary of the fraternity occurring in 1889, and report a programme of exercises suitable to the occasion, for the action of the forty-seventh annual convention."

The following officers were elected : Hon. John W. Herron, John I. Covington, and Gen. R. W. Smith, directors for three years ; J. Cal Hanna, general secretary ; C. J. Seaman, catalogue agent ; Major W. C. Ransom, transportation agent : Wm. R. Baird, historiographer ; L. C. Hascall and Marshall P. Drury, visiting officers.

The convention poem, by Dabney Marshall, was read at the banquet. Hon. D. R. Francis was master of ceremonies.

Toasts were responded to by J. Cal Hanna, Major W. C. Ransom, Gen. R. W. Smith, Dabney Marshall, George R. Lockwood, Walter B. Douglas, W. S. Jones, Chambers Baird, Jr., B. H. Charles, Jr., C. D. Roy, J. R. Montgomery, W. P. Kennett, and George F. Saal.

### 1885-'86.

In 1885-'86 the general secretary had as alumni secretary Major W. C. Ransom, and as college secretary Wilby G. Hyde. The districts retained the former boundaries, and the following chiefs were appointed : I., Ralph K. Jones ; II., Geo. F. Saal ; III., F. M. Welsh ; IV., E. B. Pollard , V., J. B. Ellis ; VI., S. E. Greenawalt ; VII., J. G. Campbell ; VIII., D. H. Bloom ; IX., Chas. F. Scott. The board organized with the same officers as before, namely : Hon. John W. Herron, president, and Willis O. Robb, secretary, the other members being John I. Covington, Dr. Thad. A. Reamy, W. F. Boyd, Hon. Peleg Emory Aldrich, Gen. R. W. Smith, and John Reily Knox. John I. Covington was re-elected general treasurer.

Frank M. Joyce was retained as business manager of the magazine. Eugene Wambaugh became editor, with F. W. Shepardson, W. C. Sprague and Richard Lee Fearn as his associates. The magazine became a monthly again. The dog, dragon, and owl on the cover were laid aside, and a blue cover with table of contents on the outside was substituted. In other respects the appearance, arrangement, and typography remained as before.

Late in 1885 the general secretary published in book form the constitution, the laws, and the alumni chapter by-laws, with all amendments to date, making a convenient compendium of Beta Theta Pi law.

As directed by the St. Louis convention, the petition from the Ohio State University was submitted to the chapters. The petition being granted, the chapter was provisionally established on December 11th, 1885, upon the occasion of the third Ohio re-union. The charter members had belonged to a local society, the Phi Alpha. Several had formerly been members of our chapters at other colleges, and a few had been initiated by the Ohio Wesleyan chapter under a dispensation.

### CONCLUSION.

The Chicago convention of 1881 marks the dividing line between two very different periods of our history. The few years ending with that convention were distinguished by rapid and almost dramatic extension, and also by the withdrawal of our weakest chapters. The years that have followed have been as different as can be conceived. There is no wisdom in debating which of the two periods was the more beneficial to the fraternity; for each period was absolutely necessary to our proper development.

Any one who has paid even the slightest attention to the details given in the preceding notes has perceived the extraordinary advance since the convention of 1881. The advance is not to be seen in figures. The increase from a membership of just four thousand, as the figures stood when we met at Chicago, to a membership of five thousand and two hundred, as the figures read to-day, is the very last and least item to which one would call attention. Nor is the increased length of the list of chapters a matter of importance. What we are proud of is the high standard of our work. We have rejected a score of petitions. The chapters established have been few; they have been placed in none but the best colleges; and they have been composed of none but desirable men. In each case a charter has been refused until a careful investigation on the spot has demonstrated that there was no danger in granting the petition. The existing chapters have been carefully watched by the chiefs, by the general secretary, and by the board of directors; so carefully, indeed, that the word of warning has always been given in time, and therefore it has been unnecessary to withdraw even one charter. The interest of the alumni has been kept alive by annual re-unions for New England, Ohio, and Indiana, not to mention numerous other gatherings. A wholly new means of perpetuating the usefulness of the fraternity among the alumni has been afforded by the Beta Theta Pi alumni club at Wooglin-on-Chautauqua Lake. Yet, why multiply words? Why go on to speak of the catalogue of 1881, of the magazine, of the development in the laws, of the improvements in methods of administration? The preceding notes have already shown clearly enough that in every department of work the years from 1881 to 1886 have seen an advance.

# THE YOUNGER MEMBERS.

A CATALOGUE OF MEMBERS ADMITTED SINCE THE CONVENTION OF 1881, WITH

NOTES AS TO COLLEGES AND CHAPTERS.

## AMHERST CHAPTER.

(The Beta Iota, at Amherst College, Amherst, Mass.)

Amherst College was founded in 1821. It has twenty-two professors and eleven other instructors. The students usually number about three hundred and fifty. The only department is the regular college course of four years. Almost all of the students are candidates for A. B., but a very few are candidates for S. B., and during the latter years of the regular course there is considerable freedom in choice of studies. The standard is high. Amherst was the first college to lay stress upon physical training. It was also the first college to place in the hands of an undergraduate senate a great part of the college discipline. The college is conservative, refusing to admit women, and still giving the classics their ancient place. It is not a state institution; and it is not sectarian, although it is, practically, controlled by orthodox Congregationalists. The gymnasium, the art gallery, and the library are well worth seeing; and the last is one of the few college libraries that are actually accessible and useful.

The eight fraternities, named in the order of establishment, are Alpha Delta Phi, Psi Upsilon, Delta Kappa Epsilon, Delta Upsilon, Chi Psi, Chi Phi, Beta Theta Pi, and Theta Delta Chi. Chapters are, generally, large, varying from twenty-five to forty. It is the custom of fraternity men to live in chapter houses, rather than in the regular college dormitories. That fraternities are recognized as valuable is shown by the following extract from President Julius H. Seelye's circular letter to the Amherst alumni, dated November, 1884: "The society houses present in all respects a desirable feature in our college life. They are well managed. The students who occupy them are careful and orderly. No houses in the village are more attractive, and no households conducted with more propriety. The general tone of the college is such that any society which should tolerate disorderly or demoralizing ways would lose not only its name, but its position and power in the college. So long as the moral sentiment of the college remains as it is, the healthy rivalry for college influence will require every society to be on the side of good order. If any member of a society has bad habits, his society, instead of favoring these, is likely to prove one of the strongest agencies in their removal. We find, therefore, that the actual influence of the societies is salutary."

The Beta Iota of Beta Theta Pi was established on the twelfth day of October, 1883, the petition having been granted by the Saratoga convention. The petitioners were the members of the Torch and Crown, a local society founded in 1878, and the charter allowed the initiation of all active or alumni members of that society, as the alumni joined with the active members in asking a charter. The membership is usually twenty-five. The corresponding secretaries have been T. C. Elliott, E. S. Damon, S. S. Parks, and R. M. Palmer. In 1884–'85 T. C. Elliott, one of the charter members, was chief of the district. The representatives at the Wooglin convention were T. C. Elliott and W. E. Russell.

### XLV.—The Founders.

WILLIAM SIDNEY BOARDMAN, '81. Student at Harvard Medical School. Home address, Newburyport, Mass.; temporary address, 8 Ashburton Place, Boston, Mass.

GEORGE RICHARDSON DICKINSON, '81. Phi Beta Kappa; Kellogg fifteen; at Yale Theological School. Home address, Cleveland, O.; temporary address, 95 W. Divinity Hall. New Haven, Conn.

WILLIAM ELIAS HINCHLIFF, '81. Kellogg

fifteen; Kellogg five; Hyde six: wholesale brick dealer. 332 Fulton street, Chicago, Ill.

LEANDER HAMILTON M'CORMICK, '81. At Columbia Law School, 126 Rush street, Chicago, Ill.

JOHN VAN BEUREN SCARBOROUGH, '81. P. O. box. 1123, Cincinnati, O.

FREDERICK WILLIAM SEARS, '81. Keeler's Bay, Vt.

ARTHUR PRESTON SMITH, '81. Keeler's Bay, Vt.

EDSON DWINELL HALE, '82. Kellogg fifteen; Hardy eight and first prize; Phi Beta Kappa philosophy prize; teacher in Hopkins Academy, Oakland, Cal.; former address, Stowe, Vt.

CHARLES EDWARD OSGOOD NICHOLS, '82. Teacher. Lock box 288, Sing Sing, N. Y.; former address, Haverhill, Mass.

GEORGE WALDO REED, '82. Hardy eight; at Hartford Theological Seminary. Home, Pittsfield, Mass., temporary address, Hosmer Hall, Hartford, Conn.

WATSON LEWIS SAVAGE, '82. Physician in Long Island Hospital. 166 State street, Brooklyn, N. Y.; former address, Cromwell, Conn.

WILLIAM HAVEN THOMPSON, '82. Phi Beta Kappa. Sudbury, Mass.

JACOB PAISLEY WHITEHEAD, '82. Kellogg fifteen and five; president of Social Union; teacher. Wealaka, Ind. Ter.; former address, Hillsboro, Ill.

EVERETT ANDERSON ABORN, '83. Former address, Ellington, Conn.; present address, Lake Forest, Ill.

CLINTON JIRAH BACKUS, '83. Teacher. Address, Baldwin School, Summit avenue, St. Paul, Minn.; former address, Chaplin, Conn.

ALMON JESSE DYER, '83. Hardy six; Glee Club; Phi Beta Kappa; at Hartford Theological Seminary. Cummington, Mass.

FRANK HERBERT FITTS, '83. Manufacturing chemist. 27 Kilby street, Boston, Mass.; former address, Walpole, Mass.

EDWIN FOWLER, '83. Phi Beta Kappa; Hyde fifteen; civil engineer; Emporia, Kansas; former address, Gouverneur, N. Y.

ISAAC FINNEY SMITH, '83. Kellogg fifteen; teacher. 114 Academy street, Poughkeepsie, N. Y.; former address, Provincetown, Mass.

WILLIAM WOOLSEY SCARBOROUGH. Honorary member of Torch and Crown. P. O. box 1123, Cincinnati, O.

WALTER STODDARD BUFFUM, '84. Hyde fifteen. 2123 Fifth avenue, New York, N. Y.; former address, Winchester, N. H.

GEORGE POMEROY EASTMAN, '84. Phi Beta Kappa; teacher. Buffalo, N. Y.; former address, Framingham, Mass.

HENRY DAVID JOHN GARDNER, '84. Ball team; at Hartford Theological Seminary. Hosmer Hall, Hartford, Conn.; former address, Buckingham, Conn.

DANIEL LYMAN GIFFORD, '84. Social Union eight. 1060 N. Halsted street, Chicago, Ill.; former address, Mendota, Ill.

ALBERT HUMPHREY PRATT, '84. Los Angeles, Cal.

GEORGE FOSTER PRENTISS, '84. Glee club; Kellogg fifteen. Home address, Windham, Vt.; temporary address, 49 E. Divinity Hall, New Haven, Conn.

JAMES HAZEN TUFTS, '84. Highest possible rank in freshman year; second Greek prize freshman year; Kellogg fifteen; Walker mathematical prize; Sophomore Latin prize; foot-ball team; Hardy prize; Hyde fifteen; position on commencement stage; Phi Beta Kappa; tutor in mathematics. Amherst, Mass.; former address, Monson, Mass.

THOMPSON COIT ELLIOTT. '85. Glee club; corresponding secretary and chief district. Emporia, Kansas; former address, Newington, Conn.

WILLIAM ADELBERT GORDON, '85. Grand Forks, Dak.; former address, 13 E. Fourteenth street, New York, N. Y.

FREDERICK WILLIAM PHELPS, '85. Sophomore Latin prize; Phi Beta Kappa; on commencement stage; teacher. Topeka, Kansas; former address, Erving, Mass.

WARREN EDWARD RUSSELL, '85. Member of the Beta Alpha. Massillon, O.

THEODORE WOOLSEY SCARBOROUGH, '85. Foot-ball team; college senate. Home address, P. O. box 1123, Cincinnati, O.; temporary address, care Q. and C. R. R., Meridian, Miss.

ELISHA MACE STEVENS, '85. Kellogg fifteen; Phi Beta Kappa; member of Rho. P. O. box 100, Minneapolis, Minn.

ARTHUR FAIRBANKS STONE, '85. President of Social Union; Phi Beta Kappa; editor on Hampshire Herald. Northampton, Mass.; former address, St. Johnsbury, Vt.

JAMES EATON TOWER, '85. Grove orator; editor of Homestead, Springfield, Mass., former address, North Brookfield, Mass.

EDWIN BURNS WOODIN, '85. Phi Beta Kappa; foot ball-team; teacher. Talequah, Ind. Ter.; former address, Amherst, Mass.

EDWIN STETSON DAMON, '86. Cor. sec.; editor Olio. Plymouth, Mass.

GEORGE CLINTON GOODWIN, '86. Lexington, Mass.

SAMUEL SHAW PARKS, '86. Kellogg. fifteen; Palmer, Mass.

WILLARD HENRY POOLE, '86. Walker mathematical prize; Phi Beta Kappa. Rockland, Mass.

CLARENCE HAYWARD WHITE, '86. Second Greek prize; Phi Beta Kappa; teacher of Greek in Amherst high school. Amherst, Mass.; former address, Raynham, Mass.

WILLIAM FAIRFIELD WHITING, '86. President foot-ball association; on foot ball-team. Holyoke, Mass.

HAMLIN AVERY WHITNEY, '86. South Gardner, Mass.

ALBERT EDWARDS WILBAR, '86. Taunton, Mass.

GEORGE COOPER DEAN, '87. Holbrook, Mass.

GEORGE NELSON GODDARD, '87. Hopedale, Mass.

CHARLES BENJAMIN STEVENS, '87. On Kellogg fifteen; Olio editor. Worcester, Mass.

EDWARD PICKETT VANDERCOOK, '85. Member of the Rho. Evanston, Ill.

XLV.

WARREN DANIEL FORBES, '86. Left college at the end of sophomore year; temporary address, Shelburne. Falls, Mass.; permanent address, Buckland, Mass.

ROBERT MANNING PALMER, '87. Corresponding secretary; glee club; leader of banjo club. Boston, Mass.

### XLVI.

HAROLD LEE JACOBS, '88, Akron, O.
LUCIUS ETHAN JUDSON, '88, Ball nine.
Painesville, O.
CHARLES BEEBE RAYMOND, '86. Akron, O.
JOHN EDWIN SMITH, '88. Foot-ball team.
Worcester, Mass.
GEORGE PALMER STEEL, '88. Foot-ball
team. Painesville, O.
CHARLES BARROWS WILBAR, '88. Taunton,
Mass.
HERBERT PEKIN WOODIN, '88. Held position on freshman Kellogg fifteen for prize speaking. Amherst, Mass.
HOMER GARD, '88. Taking special course.
Hamilton, O.

### XLVII.

WILLARD PAYSON SMITH, '88. Dunkirk,
N. Y.
JAMES CHAMBERS, JR., '89 Brooklyn, N. Y.
HENRY ARNOLD COOKE, '89. North Brookfield, Mass.
ROBERT HOLMES CUSHMAN, '89. Monson,
Mass.
BRANDON RHODEHAMEL MILLIKIN, '89.
Hamilton, O.
CHARLES DICKINSON PHELPS, '89. Erving,
Mass.

# BELOIT CHAPTER.

## [The Chi, at Beloit College, Beloit, Wis.]

Beloit College offers two courses of study, the classical and the philosophical, each being composed of prescribed work. The faculty is composed of nine professors and one assistant professor, and there are several other instructors. There are usually about seventy students in the college classes and about one hundred in the preparatory department. Women are not admitted. The college was founded in 1847 and is controlled by the Presbyterians and Congregationalists. *The Round Table* is published every other Friday of the collegiate year, by the Archaean Union. Its editorships are filled by semi-annual elections.

Beta Theta Pi, Phi Kappa Psi, and Sigma Chi are the fraternities. The average membership is ten. For many years there was great hostility to fraternities. This hostility has disappeared in the faculty, but it is still found to some extent among the students. The fraternities do not admit preparatory students and do not enter into combinations. The rule against preparatory students is one of the conditions upon which the chapters retain the right to exist openly.

The Chi of Beta Theta Pi was founded in 1860, and is more than twenty years older than its rivals. Until some two years ago the opposition to fraternities made Chi's life precarious; but the chapter is now in good shape. Its record in scholarship is remarkable. Since the convention of 1881 the corresponding secretaries have been Horace S. Fiske, Fred S. Shepherd, Henry S. Shedd, W. A. Russell, and John R. Montgomery. The chapter was represented at the convention of 1881 by C. B. McGenniss and C. J. Robertson, and at that of 1885 by John R. Montgomery.

### Admitted since August, 1881.

#### XLIV.

HENRY SPRAGUE SHEDD, '86. Bridgman prize; Archaean debater; secretary of Wisconsin State Oratorical Association; associate editor of *Whitewater* (Wis.) *Register:* corresponding secretary; now at university of Wisconsin and member of Alpha Pi. Whitewater, Wis.

HIRAM DELOS DENSMORE, '86. Archaean debater; distinguished oration for junior exhibition; exchange editor *Round Table:* home contest speaker; president Archaean union. Delavan, Wis.

WILLIAM ARTHUR RUSSELL, '87. On ball nine; freshman declaimer; vice-president of Wisconsin State Oratorical Association; Archaean debater; financial manager of *Round Table:* distinguished oration for junior exhibition; literary editor *Round Table;* cor. sec.; historian of Chi. Rochester, Wis.

JAMES ROOD ROBERTSON, '86. Personal editor *Round Table;* freshman declaimer; Archaean debater; Bridgman prize; distinguished oration for junior exhibition; home contest speaker. 121¹ S. Winnebago street, Rockford, Ill.

#### XLV.

WAYLAND SAMUEL AXTELL, '86. Distinguished oration for junior exhibition; acting president of Archaean Union. Evansville, Wis.

SAMUEL ROBERT SLAYMAKER, '86. Was member of Rho. Beloit, Wis.

BENJAMIN GEORGE BLEASDALE, '87. Teacher. Janesville, Wis.

JOHN ROGERSON MONTGOMERY, '87. Waterman prize; Archaean debater; personal editor of *Round Table;* cor. sec. 478 N. State street, Chicago, Ill.

REV. FRANK BUFFINGTON VROOMAN, '87. Lecturer with Slayton Lyceum Bureau of Chicago; student at Chicago Theological Seminary; clergyman. 145 Kansas avenue, Topeka, Kans.

#### XLVI.

HERBERT CUTLER BROWN, '87. Junior exhibition poet. Hyde Park, Ill.

HENRY HUNTINGTON SWAIN, A. B. '84. Local editor *Round Table:* Archaean debater; exchange editor *Round Table;* Bridgman prize; distinguished oration for junior exhibition; editor-in-chief *Round Table;* Beloit representative at state oratorical contest, 1884; professor of mathematics in Straight University. Straight University, New Orleans, La.

SAMUEL OTIS DAUCHY, '87. Archaean debater; local editor *Round Table.* La Salle avenue, Chicago, Ill.

FRANK DYER JACKSON, Ph. B.'84. Financial manager *Round Table:* Archaean debater; distinguished oration for junior exhibition; missionary prize essay; clerk judiciary committee of Wisconsin assembly, 1885; assistant principal of high school. Janesville, Wis.

JAMES ALEXANDER LYMAN, '88. Archaean debater. Bradford, Ill.

HARRY MORROW HYDE, '88. Archaean debater; Archaean poet. Freeport, Ill.

WILLIAM JUDSON BROWN, '87. Distinguished oration for junior exhibition. Batavia, Ill.

#### XLVII.

OTIS CALVIN OLDS, '86. Lewis prize; local editor *Round Table:* Archaean debater; Bridgman prize; missionary prize essay; home contest speaker. Clinton, Wis.

FRANK HENRY CHASE, '86. Archaean debater; Latin oration for junior exhibition. Cherry Valley, Ill.

SAMUEL MORGAN BUSHNELL, '88. Rockford, Ill.

GEORGE ALBERT CHASE, '89. Cherry Valley, Ill.

ARTHUR HENRY ARMSTRONG, '89. Whiteman prize. 218 Ogden avenue, Chicago, Ill.

# BETHANY CHAPTER.

## (The Psi, at Bethany College, Bethany, W. Va.)

At Bethany College there are usually about ninety students, including ten or fifteen women. The faculty consists of five professors. Degrees are given in arts and in science. The courses of study requisite for a degree are composed of prescribed studies; but, after the fashion of many colleges, the student is permitted to take his studies in almost any order that his necessities require; for example, he may be a sophomore in Latin while he is a junior in mathematics. The college was founded in 1841 and for some time was under the care of Alexander Campbell, the first leader of the religious denomination called Disciples. It is the chief educational institution of that denomination, and accordingly draws its students from many states.

The only fraternities are Delta Tau Delta and Beta Theta Pi. The ordinary membership of each chapter is from ten to fifteen. This is the parent chapter of Delta Tau Delta.

The Psi of Beta Theta Pi was founded in 1861. Its corresponding secretaries since the Chicago convention of 1881 have been L. B. Mertz, E. H. Miller, W. S. St. Clair, A. J. Colborn, Jr., W. McElroy, and W. C. Payne. The representatives at the convention of 1881 were H. G. Niles and M. C. Burt; at that of 1884, A. J. Colborn, Jr., L. B. Mertz, and J. A. Beall; and at that of 1885, J. F. Witmer.

### Admitted since August, 1881.

#### XLIII.

FRANCIS MARION KIMMELL. Somerset, Pa.

WILBUR BURGES LOWE. In business at Shelby, O.

HEBER REGINALD BROWN. Shelby, O.

ANDREW JACKSON COLBORN, JR., A. B. '84. Editor-in-chief of *Bethany Collegian*; valedictorian of American literary society, also valedictorian of his class; took second honors; assistant clerk house representatives Pennsylvania; lawyer. Somerset, Pa.

CORNELIUS SHAENFELD. Elmore, O.

ARTHUR LYMAN WRIGHT. Elmore, O.

#### XLIV.

WILLIAM HENRY WOLF, B. S. '85. Class poet; orator American literary society. Editor *Bethany Collegian*; teacher. Bridgeport, O.

FRANKLIN PIERCE ST. CLAIR. Professor mathematics and Latin in Hamilton Female College. Lexington, Ky.

ROGER HANSON LILLARD, B. S. '84. Manufacturer. Lawrenceburg, Ky.

REV. CHARLES GEORGE BRELOS, B. A. '84. Orator of American literary society. Buffalo, N. Y.

EMMETT AUSTIN HALL. Folks Station, O.

WILLIAM HENRY McELROY, A. B. '85. Editor-in-chief of *Bethany Collegian*; valedictorian of American literary society; first honors and Greek oration at graduation. Howard, O.

WALLACE CLAIRE PAYNE, '86. Anniversarian and twenty-second February orator, American Literary Institute; tutor in mathematics; editor *Bethany Collegian*; cor. sec.; South Bend, Ind.

ROBERT HAMILTON DEVINE. 4046 Jacob street. Wheeling, W. Va.

JOHN BROWN WILSON, B. S. '85. First honors in scientific course; orator American literary society; studying law. Wheeling, W. Va.

JAMES ANDREW HOPKINS MERTZ, B. S. '85. Chemist in Benwood Iron Works. Bellaire, O.

JAMES EDWIN ATKINSON. Clinton, Mo.

ALEXANDER McKINNEY. Clerk in custom house. Cleveland, O.

FRANK WARRINER. Studying pharmacy in New York City. Kansas City, Mo.

#### XLV.

NORMAN ARTER PHILIPS. Student at Harvard University. New Castle, Pa.

GEORGE BENJAMIN STACY. Now at Richmond Col., and member of Alpha Kappa. 406 W. Cary street, Richmond, Va.

WILLIAM HENRY MOONEY, B. S. '84. Teacher. La Grange, O.

LEWIS CASS WOOLERY, A. B. '84. First honors in classical course; professor in Bethany College. Bethany, W. Va.; former address, Antioch Mills, Ky.

MILES GRANT BAXTER, A. B. '85. Teacher of phonography. Hopedale, O.

#### XLVI.

EDWIN E. CURRY. Orator of freshman class. New Lisbon, O.

HARRY HAMPTON RUMBLE. Home, Lowell, O.; present address, Beverly, O.

#### XLVII.

ALVIN LINCOLN WHITE, '86. Orator of junior class; teacher. Bethesda, O.

W. KENT PENDLETON, JR., '88. Bethany, W. Va.

FRANK SHERMAN ISRAEL, '88. Beallsville, O.

JOHN COLEMAN REID, '87. Twenty-second orator Neatrophian literary society. Mt. Sterling, Ky.

HENRY REID BRIGHT, '87. Mt. Sterling, Ky.

## BOSTON CHAPTER.

[The Upsilon, at Boston University, Boston, Mass.]

The college department of Boston University is overshadowed by the professional schools. While the attendance upon the schools of law and medicine and theology is in the aggregate usually more than three hundred and fifty, the attendance upon the college of liberal arts rarely exceeds one hundred and forty. Women are admitted to all departments. The course of study in the college is largely elective. The university is under Methodist control; but, because of its admitting women and because of its having the only medical school in New England not controlled by the so-called regular school of physicians, it has interested many persons outside of the Methodist denomination, and has been prevented from becoming merely sectarian. The theological school is, however, strictly devoted to the Methodist Episcopal church. The university was founded in 1869. It has ample means. The buildings stand in the heart of the city, and there are no dormitories except in connection with the theological school.

Beta Theta Pi and Theta Delta Chi are the fraternities, both founded in 1876. The average size of chapters is about fifteen. Theta Delta Chi usually has considerably more than that number.

The Upsilon has always confined its membership to the college department, although the professional schools offer a tempting field. Upsilon is careful in selecting men, and almost every one of its members has remained in college until graduation. The chapter has been active in fraternity work. The corresponding secretaries since the convention of 1881 have been Chas. F. Waterhouse, Jas. E. Lawrence, Wm. B. Snow, Walter S. Little, J. H. McKenzie, George E. Whitaker, and Wm. M. Warren. The representatives at the convention of 1881 were A. C. Poole and A. H. Flack; at that of 1882, C. F. Waterhouse and A. C. Poole; at that of 1883, A. H. Flack and L. C. Hascall; and that of 1884, J. H. Kenzie. L. C. Hascall was visiting officer for 1883-84, 1884-85, and 1885-86.

### Admitted since August, 1881.

#### XLIII.

WALTER SANDERSON LITTLE, '85. Cor. sec.; wholesale boot and shoe business. Permanent address, Wellsley, Mass.; temporary address, 292 Devonshire street, Boston Mass.

#### XLIV.

GEORGE EDGAR WHITAKER, '85. *Beacon* manager; cor. sec.; astronomical computer. Permanent address, Worcester, Mass.; temporary, 22 Aldersey St., Somerville, Mass.

WILLIAM BRACKET SNOW, '85. Commencement speaker; business manager *Beacon*; cor. sec.; sub-master in the English high school, Boston. Stoneham, Mass.

ORDELL HERCULES POWERS, '84. Publishing business. 5 and 7 East Fourth street, New York, N. Y.

JOSEPH CLARENCE HAGEN, '86. Commencement speaker; editor *Beacon*; president of the "*Deutsches Kraenzchen*"; teacher at Comer's Commercial College. Permanent address, E. Marshfield, Mass.

#### XLV.

WILLIS BRECKENRIDGE HOLCOMBE, '86. Left college in '84 to study in Germany. Gottingen is his present address; permanent address, Richmond, Indiana.

BERNHARD BERENSON, '87. Went to Harvard in '85 to pursue special course. 11 Minot street, Boston, Mass.

JOHN HEYWARD McKENZIE, '84. Cor. sec.;

Ph. D. Teacher in Wesleyan college, Cincinnati, O.

WILLIAM MARSHALL WARREN, '87. Cor. sec. 329 Broadway, Cambridgeport, Mass.

#### XLVI.

WALTER PERKINS TAYLOR, '84. Andover Theological Seminary. Andover, Mass.; home address, Charlottetown. P. E. I.

WALTER EDWARD HARRISON MASSEY, '87. With Massey manufacturing company, Toronto, Ont.

CLIFF RODGERS RICHARDS, '88. E. Marshfield, Mass.

LEWIS NEWELL CUSHMAN, '87. East Boston, Mass.

ERNEST WILLIAM BRANCH, '88. Granby, Mass.

#### XLVII.

LAWRENCE BAKER GREENWOOD, '88. Everett, Mass.

ERNEST AVERY JOHNSTON, '88. Dorchester, Mass.

GEORGE AINSWORTH DUNN, '89. Gardner, Mass.

BENJAMIN COLE GILLIS, '89. Mechanicsville, Vt.

LINVILLE HEBER WARDWELL, '89. Beverly, Mass.

THOMAS WHITESIDE, '89. Chicopee, Mass.

#### XLVIII.

JESSE GRANT CRAMER, '89. Auburndale, Mass.

# BROWN CHAPTER.

Brown University has seventeen professors and five other instructors. The students number, usually, between two hundred and fifty and three hundred. Women are not admitted. The popular course is the one leading to A. B., although there are a few in the Ph. B. course. Beginning with junior year, about one-third of the work is elective. Rhode Island's share of the national land grant for agricultural and mechanical colleges was by the legislature assigned to Brown, but that fact has not appreciably affected the courses of study. In fact, the professor of agricultural zoology is about the only visible mark of the agricultural and mechanical department. The university was founded in 1764. It is governed by a board of trustees, in which body various religious denominations have a certain representation that was long ago fixed upon; but the majority of the trustees must be Baptists, and so must the president of the university; and this is the reason why Brown, though really unsectarian, is always considered a Baptist institution.

The fraternities in the order of original foundation are Alpha Delta Phi, Delta Phi, Psi Upsilon, Beta Theta Pi, Delta Kappa Epsilon, Zeta Psi, Theta Delta Chi, Delta Upsilon, and Chi Phi. The membership of prosperous chapters ranges from fifteen to thirty. There are no chapter houses.

The Kappa, founded in 1847, was revived in 1880. The chapter usually numbers about seventeen. The corresponding secretaries since the convention of 1881 have been E. B. Harvey, A. D. Cole, A. P. Sumner, Jos. H. Ward, Harry T. Sherman, Geo. H. Crooker. John T. Blodgett, of Kappa, was chief of the district from 1881 to 1883. At the convention of 1881 the representatives were H. S. Babcock, W. H. Tolman, and A. P. Hoyt, the last being one of the vice-presidents; at that of 1882, H. S. Babcock and C. H. J. Douglas, the former being a vice-president and being also the convention poet; at that of 1883, E. P. Allen, E. B. Harvey, and A. P. Sumner; at that of 1884, A. P. Sumner; and at that of 1885, W. F. Angell. The Providence alumni chapter, which is chiefly composed of members of Kappa, has had, at various conventions, representatives who are not included in the foregoing list.

## Admitted since August, 1881.

### XLIII.

CLARENCE OTIS WILLIAMS, A. B. '85. Phi Beta Kappa; instructor. Permanent address, New Hampton, N. H.; present address, 31 Hammond street, Providence, R. I.

ARTHUR PRESTON SUMNER, A. B. '85. *Liber* editor; cor. sec.; law student. 466 Broad street. Providence, R. I.

EDWIN THOMAS BANNING. '85. Left college in junior year; draughtsman. 45 Westminster street, Providence, R. I.

AMORY PRESCOTT FOLWELL, A. B. '85. Second Hartshorn prize in mathematics; studying law. Permanent address, Brooklyn, N. Y.; present address, 749 Tremont street, Boston, Mass.

JOSEPH WOOD FREEMAN, A. B. '85. Received commencement appointment; editor of Central Falls *Visitor*. Central Falls, R. I.

CLIFFORD PHETTEPLACE SEAGRAVE, A. B. '85. Ball nine, and captain; class day marshal in 1884; manufacturer. 119 Benefit street, Providence, R. I.

HORATIO GATES WOOD, A. B. '85. Speaker at class tree; traveling in Europe. 34 Mill street, Newport, R. I.

### XLIV.

NORMAN GUNDERSON, '86. Class day marshal in 1885; ball nine, and captain. 35 Pitman street, Providence, R. I.

JOSEPH HOOKER WARD, '86. Editor of *Brunonian* for '84, '85, '86. President of glee club; cor. sec.; vice-president of Hammer and Tongs in junior year. Middletown, R. I.

FRANCIS WAYLAND SHEPARDSON, A. B. '83. Member of the Alpha Eta; instructor. Granville, O.

ARTHUR YOUNG FORD, A. B. '84. Phi Beta Kappa; member of the Epsilon; received commencement appointment; editor of *Brunonian*. Editor at Owensboro, Ky.

*LOUIS SHIEL, '86. Editor of *Brunonian*; ball nine. Died in 1884; home was Philadelphia, Penn.

### XLV.

EDWARD ELISHA PIERCE, A. B. '77. Wholesale grocer. 19 and 20 Canal street, Providence, R. I.

GEORGE WASHINGTON WILLIS, '86. Chairman for *Liber* board for 1886; on ball nine. 38 Laycock street, Alleghany City, Penn.

HARRY FREDERICK COLWELL, '87. Leader of Symphony Society; theatrical director of Hammer and Tongs. 58 Bowen street, Providence, R. I.

GEORGE HAZARD CROOKER, '87. *Liber* editor for 1887; on ball nine; vice-president of Hammer and Tongs. 58 Benefit street, Providence, R. I.

### XLVI.

CHARLES ENGS LAWTON, '86. Newport, R. I.
FRANCIS JOSEPH BELCHER, '88. 19 Slater Hall. Providence, R. I.
HUGH LECKIS CATTANNACH, '88. Angell Place, Providence, R. I.
HARRY TUCK SHERMAN, '88. Cor. sec.; glee club. Barrett House, New York, N. Y.

### XLVII.

GEORGE WALLACE HUTCHINSON, '88. Ball nine; now student at Princeton. Home address, Windsor, N. J.
HENRY JOHNS RHETT, Ph. B. '85. Third Carpenter prize in elocution; captain of foot-ball team; ball nine. With Providence Locomotive Works. 85 Benevolent street, Providence. R. I.
FREDERICK HUNTINGTON BRIGGS, '89. 449 Beacon street, Boston. Mass.
ROBERT LINCOLN SPENCER, '89. Ball nine; secretary glee club. 35 Sycamore street, Providence, R. I.
CHARLES FRANCIS SMITH, '89. Jamestown, N. Y.
CHARLES AARON SAWYER, '89. Malone, N. Y.
ARTHUR FRANKLIN CLARK, '89, Ball nine. 10 Paine street. Providence, R. I.

## UNIVERSITY OF CALIFORNIA CHAPTER.

[The Omega, at the University of California, Berkeley, Cal.]

The University of California is controlled by the state. Its buildings and grounds are worth a million dollars; and the productive funds amount to almost two million. The university was founded in 1868, and absorbed the College of California, which was founded in 1855. In the undergraduate department there are courses leading to degrees in arts, letters, philosophy, and science. The museums, laboratories, and libraries are extremely valuable, being conducted upon the most modern plan. In the undergraduate department there are about two hundred and fifty students, including about fifty women. There are eighteen professors and fourteen other instructors. The professional schools are in San Francisco. They are devoted to medicine, dentistry, pharmacy, and law, with an aggregate attendance of about two hundred and sixty. The officers of instruction in the professional schools number fifty-seven. The university will soon have an observatory with a telescope more powerful than any heretofore made, the cost to be $700,000.

The fraternities are Zeta Psi, Phi Delta Theta, Chi Phi, Delta Kappa Epsilon, Beta Theta Pi. A chapter's membership varies from ten to twenty. Until recently there was much opposition to fraternities. The anti-fraternity law was successfully fought in the courts, and public opposition ceased four or five years ago. One of the anti-fraternity organs that were for a long while supported by students has ceased publication, and the other is no longer an anti-fraternity journal.

Omega is so remote from the main body of the fraternity that, though founded in 1879, it has been represented in only two conventions. Guy C. Earl was at the convention of 1881; and at the convention of 1884, Chas. S. Wheeler, C. H. Forbes, and Guy Wilkinson were present, Wheeler being one of the vice-presidents. When the chapter is not represented by delegates, it sends a letter or a telegram, in order that the lack of representation may not be construed to be caused by lack of interest in the fraternity. The corresponding secretaries since the convention of 1881 have been W. W. Deamer, Chas. S. Wheeler, W. Palache, C. A. Ramm, and Finlay Cook. In 1883-'84 Wheeler was chief of the district.

**Admitted since August, 1881.**

**XLIII.**

STAFFORD WALLACE AUSTIN, '86. President of the day, Charter day, 1886. Hilo, Hawaii, Hawaiian Islands.

SAMUEL HUBBARD, JR., '86. Left college in 1883. Yakima, Wash. T.

ANDREW D. SCHINDLER, '83. U. S. coast survey. Berkeley, Cal.

ROBERT CHESTER TURNER, '86. Made welcome address to President Holden on behalf of students, January, 1886. 1052 Poplar street, Oakland, Cal.

EDWARD STAFFORD WARREN, '85. President junior day. Haywards, Almeda county, Cal.

**XLIV.**

JOHN WARREN DUTTON, '86. Left college in 1884. 1328 California street, San Francisco, Cal.

GUY WILKINSON, '86. Early English prize. Address, care of M. Carter, 61½ Broad street, Boston, Mass.

RICHARD BOLTON HELLMAN, '86. Left college in 1883. At present in Peru; former address, 1212 Geary street, San Francisco, Cal.

WHITNEY PALACHE, '87. Left college in 1885. Berkeley, Cal.

WILFRIED BELA WELLMAN, '86. Left college in 1885. Fruitvale, Alameda county, Cal.

**XLV.**

JOHN FRANCIS DAVIS, A. B., Harvard, '81. Took post-graduate course at University of California; law student; traveling in Europe. Home address, San Francisco, Cal.

FREDERICK CHESTER TURNER, '87. Member of base-ball nine and foot-ball team. 1420 Eighth street, Oakland, Cal.

JOHN CUSHING DOONIN, '87. Berkeley, Cal.

ARTHUR JAMES THATCHER, '87. Hopland, Mendocino county, Cal.

GEORGE WASHINGTON DUTTON, '87. Left college in 1884. San Rafael, Marion county, Cal.

ROBERT THOMSON STRATTON, '87. Left college in 1884. At Jefferson Medical College, Philadelphia, Pa.; permanent address, East Oakland, Cal.

GEORGE MALCOLM STRATTON, '87. 461 East Twelfth street, Oakland, Cal.

**XLVI.**

OLIVER BRYANT ELLSWORTH, '88. Niles, Alameda county, Cal.

**XLVII.**

GAILLARD STONER, '88. 2410 Washington street, San Francisco, Cal.

WILLIAM INGRAHAM KIP, '88. Base-ball nine. Berkeley, Cal.

FINLAY COOK, '88. Cor. sec. 458 Bryant street, San Francisco, Cal.

WILLIAM HANNAFORD WENTWORTH, '88. Nevada City, Cal.

CHARLES JAMES EVANS, '88. Business manager Berkeleyan. 2207 Adeline street, Oakland, Cal.

HUGH HOWELL, '89. 669 Seventeenth street, Oakland, Cal.

CLIFFORD WEBSTER BARNES, '89. 524 Downey avenue, Los Angeles, Cal.

JAMES EDGAR BEARD, '88. Napa City, Cal.

## CENTRE CHAPTER.

[The Epsilon, at the Centre College of Kentucky, Danville, Ky.]

Centre College, founded in 1819, is the most important southern institution controlled by the northern Presbyterian church. The college offers two courses, a classical and a scientific. In the college department there are six professors and about one hundred students. No institution in Kentucky sends out year by year a larger class of graduates. There is also a preparatory department.

The fraternities are Beta Theta Pi, Phi Delta Theta, Sigma Chi, and southern Kappa Alpha. The size of a chapter varies from eight to sixteen. Preparatory students are seldom admitted by any of the fraternities.

The Epsilon was founded in 1848, and has been one of the most successful chapters of Beta Theta Pi. As is the case with many other old chapters, its active membership is largely composed of the sons and brothers of former members. Since the convention of 1881 the corresponding secretaries have been H. C. Read, S. C. Jones, Lee Dunlap, S. T. Hickman, W. B. Mathews, H. L. Briggs, and W. E. Bryce. The chapter has recently had two chiefs of the district, John A. Heron in 1881–'82 and Alfred C. Downs in 1882–'83. The representatives at the convention of 1881 were B. B. Veech, G. C. Cowles, and W. H. January; at that of 1882, H. C. Read, W. B. Mathews, and G. C. Cowles; at that of 1883, B. G. Boyle; at that of 1884, B. G. Boyle, J. W. Kennedy, and J. W. Guest, Jr.; and at that of 1885, S. D. Roser and Lee Dunlap. W. H. January was song-book agent of the fraternity from 1881 to 1884, and prepared the book now in use.

### Admitted since August, 1881.

#### XLIII.

STANLEY CASS ARCHIBALD, '85. Member of the Alpha Lambda. With Procter & Gamble, Cincinnati, O.

WILLIAM HARRIS BRIGGS, '85. Danville, Ky.

HARRY LEE BRIGGS, '85. Sophomore Latin prize; February oration; cor. sec. Danville, Ky.

#### XLIV.

WILLIAM BURGESS MATHEWS, JR., '85. Valedictory; June oration; sophomore Latin prize; cor. sec. Maysville, Ky.

SEBASTIAN CHATHAM JONES, '84. Cor sec; studying at Cornell University. Home, Louisville, Ky.

SAMUEL TEBBS HICKMAN, '85. Cor. sec. With Palmer, Dodge & Co., Chicago Ill.

WASHINGTON CURRAN WHITTHORNE, '86. Columbia, Tenn.

SAMUEL DE WITT ROSER, '84. St. Louis, Mo.

LEE DUNLAP, '84. With Rice, Stix & Co., 3412 Vine st., St. Louis, Mo.

SYDNEY JOHNSTON HAYDEN, '84. Teaching in Chenault's school, Louisville, Ky.

#### XLV.

JAMES CROZIER COLEMAN, '86. Versailles, Ky.

HARRY Y. WHITTHORNE, '87. Columbia, Tenn.

CHARLES H. IRVINE, '87. Danville, Ky.

JAMES WELSH GUEST, JR., '84. February oration; studying medicine at University of Virginia. Danville, Ky.

#### XLVI.

ORVILLE TRUMAN SKILLMAN, '87. Cloverport, Ky

EUGENE FURGUSON VEST, '88. Cloverport, Ky.

GELON ROUT CRAFT, '87. Holly Springs, Miss.

GEORGE WASHINGTON BROADUS, '86. February oration. Mt. Sterling, Ky.

WILLIS SHALLCROSS MULLEN, '89. Louisville, Ky.

RICHARD GIVENS DENNY, '86. Shelby City, Ky.

OBADIAH BRUMFIELD CALDWELL, '88. Danville, Ky.

#### XLVII.

WILLIAM ELLSWORTH BRYCE, '86. February oration; cor. sec. Indianapolis, Ind.

CLARENCE MATHEWS, '88. Maysville, Ky.

WILLIAM COCHRAN, '89. June oration. Maysville, Ky.

JAMIE COCHRAN, '89. Maysville, Ky.

ROBERT ANDERSON WATTS, '89. 1216 Second street, Louisville, Ky.

## [The Alpha Alpha, at Columbia College, New York, N. Y.]

Columbia College is one of the wealthiest institutions in the United States, and also, if the students in all departments are counted, one of the largest. There are one hundred and five instructors and about fourteen hundred students. The school of arts has about two hundred and fifty students; the school of political science, about seventy; the school of mines, about two hundred and fifty; the college of physicians and surgeons, about five hundred; and the law school, about three hundred and fifty. The last two are in the front rank of professional schools. The school of mines was established for the especial purpose of giving instruction in studies pertaining to mining, but other lines of work have been added, and now the courses cover almost all branches of science. It has for twenty years been the prominent undergraduate department of the college. The school of arts, founded in 1754, and for many years the only department, is now growing in favor; and it has recently been reinforced by the founding of the school of political science. Columbia has always been under Protestant Episcopal control; but the denominational bias is not noticed except in the school of arts.

In the order of original foundation the fraternities now existing are Alpha Delta Phi, Psi Upsilon, Delta Phi, Chi Psi, Delta Psi, Phi Gamma Delta, Delta Kappa Epsilon, Zeta Psi, Beta Theta Pi, Delta Tau Delta, and Phi Delta Theta. A chapter's membership, counting all departments of the college, varies from fifteen to fifty. Initiations are generally confined to the arts and the mines.

The Alpha Alpha received a charter from the Chicago convention and on the 28th of October, 1881, was formally instituted. The corresponding secretaries have been W. A. Jones, Jr., Thos. B. Evans, C. B. Van Tuyl, and E. J. Lederle. W. R. Baird, one of the charter members, was chief of the district in 1881–'82. At the convention of 1883 the representatives were W. R. Baird and C. H. Doolittle, and that of 1884 O. E. Coles and E. W. Newton. From 1882 to 1885 W. R. Baird was one of the editors of the magazine, and since 1885 he has been historiographer.

### XLIII.—The Founders.

WILLIAM RAIMOND BAIRD, '82 law. Chief of district ; associate editor of *Beta Theta Pi;* historiographer; member of Sigma; author of *American College Fraternities;* lawyer. 243 Broadway, New York, N. Y.

WILLIAM BEEBE MIDDLETON, '83. Mines; left college 1882. 370 Adelphi street, Brooklyn, N. Y.

LOTHAR WASHINGTON FABER, '82. Mines. Left college 1882. With E. Faber, 812 Broadway, New York, N. Y.; permanent address, Port Richmond, Staten Island, N. Y.

WILLIAM ABBOTT JONES, JR., '84. Arts; studied at Gottingen; Columbia school of political science 1885; now member of '86 school of law and candidate for Ph. D. at school of political science; cor. sec. Richmond Hill, L. I., N. Y.

HENRY MESA, '82. Mines. Left college 1881. New York, N. Y.

CLINTON BRAZIL VAN TUYL, '84. Mines. Left college 1883, returned 1884, left 1885; cor. sec. Rio de Janeiro, Brazil, S. A.

CHARLES HORACE DOOLITTLE, M. E., '85. Cor. sec.; now chemist and assayer in copper and silver works. Denver, Col.

WILBUR EDGERTON SANDERS, M. E., '85. Bow oar of victorious '85 crew; now mining in Arizona. Address, Helena, Montana Territory.

### XLIII.

THOMAS BROWN EVANS, '85. Mines. Cor.

sec.; left college 1884; now candidate for Ph .D. in chemistry at the University of Erlangen, Bavaria. Clifton, Cincinnati, O.

JOHN DOWNING LOGAN, '84. Arts. Left college 1883. Greenpoint, L. I., N. Y.

HOWARD HAROLD CLEVELAND, LL. B. '82. St. Paul, Minn.

### XLIV.

DE LAGNEL BERIER, LL. B. '82. Fort Hamilton, N. Y.

OTWAY WILKINSON BALDWIN, LL. B., '83. A. B., University of Minnesota, 1881. Clear Lake, Minn.

CHARLES FREDERICK ACKERMAN, '83. Mines. Left college 1882. 54 Livingston street, Brooklyn, N. Y.

PAUL WILCOX, LL. B. '84. Member of Delta. Practicing law in New York City.

ERNST JOSEPH LEDERLE, '86. Mines. Cor. sec.; class president in 1885. Stapleton, Staten Island, N. Y.

CHARLES EDWIN PARKER, '86. Mines. Member of Alpha Nu; left college 1883; Ph. C. University of Michigan, 1885. Ottawa, Kas.

FREDERICK GROVE PADDOCK, '84 law. Left college 1883. Malone, N. Y.

FREDERICK MAYHEN THOMAS, M. E. '85. Cor. sec. Skaneateles, New York.

CHARLES EDWIN CAHOONE, '86. Mines. Left college 1883; secretary and treasurer Cahoone-Voorhees manufacturing company, Newark, N. J. Frelinghuysen avenue, Newark, N. J.

### XLV.

OLIVER EDWARD COLES, '84. Arts. Degrees of Ph. B. and A. B.; now a member of '87 law. P. O. box 262, Jersey City, N. J.

WILLIAM PAUL WILCOX, M. D. '83. Omaha, Neb.

EDWARD HERMAN BARNUM, '86. Mines. Left college 1883. 458 Pacific street. Brooklyn, N. Y.

EDWARD COHEN, A. B. '84. 305 Lexington avenue, New York, N. Y.

EDGAR STORM APPLEBY, A. B. '84. Member of '86 law. 216 W. Fifty-ninth street, New York, N. Y.

### XLVI.

FREDERICK ANTHONY BRISTOL, '87. Mines. Left college 1885. Room 23, Mannheimer Block, St. Paul, Minn.

EBEN W. NEWTON, A. B. '84. New York, N. Y.

HARRY GILBERT DARWIN, '87. Mines. Glen Ridge, N. J.

DANIEL CORY ADAMS, '87. Mines. North Plainfield, N. J.

JAMES LINCOLN HURD, '88. Mines. Dover, N. J.

### XLVII.

FRANCIS ROLLIN PERCIVAL, '86. med. Member of Beta Alpha. 89 Lexington avenue. New York. N. Y.

RUSH CLARK LAKE, '85 law. Member of Alpha Beta. Independence, Iowa.

JAMES ISHAM GILBERT, LL. B. '85. Member of Alpha Beta. Burlington, Iowa.

SAMUEL EDSON GAGE, '87. Mines. On bicycle team for intercollegiate games. Flushing, Long Island, N. Y.

JOHN ERICSSON CLUTE, '86 med. Member of Nu. Schenectady, N. Y.

WILLIAM THOMAS PARTRIDGE, '88. Mines. Artist-in-chief of *Miner*. Washington, D. C.

## CORNELL CHAPTER.

### [The Beta Delta, at Cornell University, Ithaca, N. Y.]

Cornell has about sixty instructors and six hundred students. The studies are largely elective. A majority of the students are candidates for degress in arts or philosophy or science; but there are over two hundred in the courses in architecture, engineering, and agriculture. The university was incorporated in 1865 and opened in 1868. It is not a sectarian institution; and it is not in any strict sense a state institution; for New York's share of the congressional land grant for agricultural colleges is not the principal part of the university's support, and the governor and other public officials who have seats as trustees are the minority of that board. The university campus is one of the finest in the United States. Its chief beauties are its walks, drives, and trees, and the view over Lake Cayuga.

In the order of original foundation are the fraternities are Zeta Psi, Kappa Alpha, Alpha Delta Phi, Chi Psi, Phi Kappa Psi, Delta Upsilon, Delta Kappa Epsilon, Theta Delta Chi, Phi Delta Theta, Beta Theta Pi, and Psi Upsilon. Each chapter has from ten to twenty-six members. Almost every chapter owns or rents a house.

The Beta Delta was founded in 1874. It rents a chapter house. The usual membership is fifteen. The recent corresponding secretaries were F. E. Wilcox, H. C. Elmer, H. L. Shively, J. T. Sackett, G. F. Saal, and Theodore Miller. Saal is now chief of the district. The chapter was represented at the convention of 1881 by H. F. Ehrman; at that of 1882 by H. C. Elmer and H. F. Ehrman; at that of 1883 by F. R. Percival, F. E. Wilcox, and A. A. Alling; at that of 1884 by G. F. Saal and J. T. Sackett; and at that of 1885 by G. F. Saal.

### Admitted since August, 1881.

#### XLIV.

THOMAS CORMODY, JR., 82. Lawyer. Bellona, N. Y.

CHARLES LOCKE CURTIS, A. B, '83. Editor Cornell Sun: now with Toledo Blade, Toledo, O.

WALTER FRANCIS HAMP, '85. South Pueblo, Col.

HERBERT CHARLES ELMER, A. B, '83. Woodford orator; Phi Beta Kappa; major C. U. cadets '83; junior president; cor. sec.; M. A. Johns Hopkins and member of Alpha Chi; studied philosophy at Leipzig and Bonn. Permanent address, Rushford, N. Y.; temporary address, Johns Hopkins University, Baltimore, Md.

*PATRICK JOSEPH CASEY, '82. Cornellian editor; died August 1883. Binghamton N. Y.

FRANK PERCY INGALLS, '84. Salem, Mass.

FRANK WARREN SHELDON, '86. 265 Garden street, Hoboken, N. J.

JOHN THOMSON SACKETT, '86. Business manager Cornell Sun. '85-'86. Memorial orator '86; cor. sec. 477 Greene avenue, Brooklyn, N. Y.

ARTHUR THEODORE EMORY, '86. University ball nine '83-'84; glee club. Unadilla, N. Y.

EDWARD MAGUIRE, B. S. '84. Seward, N. Y.

#### XLV.

JOHN LEONARD SOUTHWICK, Ph. B, '83. Cornell Sun '82-83; senior class prophet. Bombay, N. Y.

JOHN LOVEJOY PRATT, JR., B. L, '83. Editor Cornell Sun '82-83; memorial orator senior class; Phi Beta Kappa. Buskirks Bridge, N. Y.

FRED WISNER CARPENTER, B. C. E. '84. Permanent address, Owego, N. Y.; temporary address, Morris Docks, New York, N. Y.

FRANK ROLLIN PERCIVAL, '86. Now at College of Physicians and Surgeons, New York City. Permanent address, Summers, Ct.; temporary address, 97 Lexington avenue, New York, N. Y.

HARRY LAWRENCE SHIVELY, B. S. '84. Business manager Cornell Sun '83-'84; mid-course honors in French and German; final honors in German. Los Angeles, Cal.

CHARLES DAVID WHITE, '86. Editor Cornell Sun '84; editor Cornell Review '85; editor Cornellian; instructor in free-hand drawing at Cornell University '84-'86. Marion, N. Y.

FRANK ALVAH CONVERSE, '86. President of Cornell University Agricultural Association '84. Woodville, N. Y.

GEORGE WILLIAMSON VAN VRANKEN, Ph. B, '85. Transferred from Nu; editor Cornell Daily Sun. Lisha's Kill, N. Y.

ARTHUR CECIL COPELAND. Post-graduate in veterinary science; transferred from Alpha Psi. Monroe, Wis.

GEORGE FREDERIC SAAL, '87. Cor. sec.; chief district. 40 Ontario street, Cleveland, O.

CHARLES BALDWIN HAGADORNE, '86. Pitcher ball-nine; West Point cadet '85. Temporary address, West Point, N. Y.; permanent address, 128 E. Genung Place, Elmira, N. Y.

EDGAR BOYD McCONNELL, '87. Logansport Ind.

THOMAS WILBUR TOMLINSON, '87. Permanent address, Logansport, Ind.; temporary address. 2 Old Chamber of Commerce, Chicago, Ill.

#### XLVI.

ARTHUR HASTINGS GRANT, '87. President C. U. Christian Association '86. 132 East Twenty-fourth street, New York, N. Y.

JOHN JUDSON ASPINWALL, '87. 141 Seventh street, Buffalo, N. Y.

WILLIAM MASON HARRIS, '87. Permanent

address, Owego, N. Y.; present address, Binghamton, N. Y.

WILLIAM PARKER CUTLER, '88. Washington, D. C.

CHARLES SUMNER FOWLER, '88. Gouverneur, N. Y.

GEORGE HARRY GIBSON, '88. Peoria, Ill.

FREDERICK MARSHALL STAUNTON, '88. Charleston, Kanawha county, W. Va.

WILLIAM HENRY PFAU, '88. Hamilton, O.

THEODORE MILLER, '88. Editor *Cornell Sun* '85-'86; cor. sec. Antwerp, N. Y.

SEBASTIAN CHATHAM JONES, '87. Member of Epsilon. Aurora, N. Y.

### XLVII.

HENRY H. HUMPHREY, A. B. Ohio University, '84; transferred from Beta Kappa. Coolville, Athens county, O.

HENRY GOLDSMITH DIMON, '87. Ball nine '85-'86. Riverhead, L. I., N. Y.

JOHN HURD DROWN, '89. 1507 Fifth street, N. W., Washington, D. C.

ALBERT HENRY WASHBURN, '89. Middleboro, Mass.

WILLIAM LOWREY COOLING, '88. Wilmington, Del.

MILO FREEMAN WEBSTER, '88. Victor, Ontario county, N. Y.

### XLVIII.

FRED WELLES HARGREAVES, '89. Wappinger's Falls, N. Y.

GEORGE BRAYTON PENNEY, '89. Ottawa, Ill.

# CUMBERLAND CHAPTER.

## [The Mu, at Cumberland University, Lebanon, Tenn.]

From 1842, the date of its foundation, to 1861, Cumberland was one of the most important universities in the south. The civil war crippled it in many respects, but it is still an important institution, for its law school still attracts students from all of the southern states, and its theological school is still the only one belonging to the Cumberland Presbyterian church. The college department is not large, but it is of good grade. The average attendance upon the several departments is as follows: college, sixty; law school, fifty; theological school, thirty-five. In these three departments there are fourteen professors. There is also a preparatory department.

Before the civil war, almost every important fraternity was represented by a chapter. Now there are only Beta Theta Pi and Sigma Alpha Epsilon.

The Mu was founded in 1854. Its membership comes largely from the professional schools and varies from fifteen to twenty-five. The recent corresponding secretaries were James C. Harris, R. W. McDonald, J. W. Caldwell, and Hallett Harding The chapter received several dispensations allowing it to elect and initiate Vanderbilt students; and the members thus initiated will be found in the Vanderbilt roll.

### Admitted since August, 1881.

#### XLIV.

JAMES CHESLEY HARRIS, '83 law. Member of the Beta Beta. Ripley, Mississippi.

JAMES PURDEY ATKINSON, '83 law. Graduate of University of Tennessee. Union, Oregon.

CHARLES EMMET PATE, '83. Editor of Student; lawyer. Memphis, Tennessee.

ALFRED HOLT CARRIGAN, JR., '83 law. A. B. Arkansas Ind. University, 1882. Washington, Arkansas.

EDWARD PINCKNEY HILL, '83 law. Graduated at Marshall in 1877, with gold medal. Marshall, Texas.

WILLIAM BRYAN HOUSTON, '83 law. San Antonio, Texas.

REED LANSDON McDONNOLD, '86. Lebanon, Tenn.

JIM FRANKLIN FOWLKES, '83 law. Bakerville, Tenn.

WENDEL SPENCE, '83 law. Austin, Texas.

BAKER ST. CLAIR RADFORD, '83 law. Hopkinsville, Ky.

BENJAMIN CHRISTIE MICKLE, '83 law. Valedictorian at Bethel College in 1879. Fulton, Ky.

C. M. TEMPLETON, '83 law. Winsborough, Tex.

CLIFTON A. GREEN, '86. Springfield, Ky.

REV. JACOB R. HODGES, '84 theo. Member of Alpha Omicron. Salado, Tex.

HORATIO HYDE PARKER, '83 law. Knoxville, Tenn.

ALBERT SUMMERFIELD DICKEY, '83 law. A. B. and valedictorian at Hiwassee College in 1879. Sweetwater, Monroe county, Tenn.

ARTHUR HENDERSON COOPER, '83 law. Marshall, Harrison county, Tex.

#### XLV.

REV. RICHARD WELBOURNE LEWIS, '85 theology. B. S. University of Tennessee, '82. Brownwood, Tex.

HON. WILLIS GOLLIDAY. Member of Mississippi Legislature.

A. B. FREEMAN. Lebanon, Tenn.

#### XLVI.

JOSEPH WEISEGER CALDWELL, '86 theo. Ex-editor and business manager of Student; was a member of Epsilon. Danville, Ky.

JAMES HENRY MILLER, '86 theology. Editor-in-chief of Student; was a member of Alpha Omicron. Da Villa, Tex.

WINSTEAD PAINE BONE, '86 theology. Business manager of Student; was a member of Alpha Omicron. La Rissa, Tex.

JEROME BOUTSFORD KERR, '85 theology. Transferred from Alpha Omicron. McKinney, Tex.

HON. WILLIAM HENRY CLARKE, '85 law. Was a member of Beta Beta; member of Legislature of Mississippi. Brandon, Miss.

ERNEST WILLIAM STEWART, '85 law. Vaden, Miss.

ALBERT DAVIS MARKS, '85 law. Practicing law at Winchester, Tenn.

SAMUEL RICHARD PACE. Irregular course. Marrowbone, Ky.

OSCAR LEE STRIBLING, '85 law. Practicing law at Tupelo, Miss.

JAMES WHITE HANDLEY, '85. M. D., Vanderbilt, 1886. Nashville, Tenn.

GEORGE BEATTY WARD, '87. Birmingham, Ala.

JOHN SAM OWSLEY, JR., '87. Stanford, Ky.

BROUSSAIS COMAN, LL. B. '85. Practicing law at Athens, Ala.

FRANK GORDON BRIDGES, '85. New Middletown, Tenn.

REV. WILLIAM DOWNY BLAIR, '85. Henderson, Ky.

JAMES SHANNON BUCHANNAN, '85. Teaching at Harpeth, Tenn.

HARRY JAMES BONE, '85 law. Practicing law at Wellington, Kas.

REV. JEFFERSON RUSSELL CRAWFORD, '85. Marrowbone. Ky.

#### XLVII.

WILLIAM LEE McCUTCHEN, '87. Pilot Grove, Mo.

CURRY KIRKPATRICK, '87. Associate editor of Student; Lebanon, Tenn.

ISAAC WILLIAM PLEASANT BUCHANAN, '85. Teaching near Lebanon, Tenn.

JOHN CREMER RITTER, '86 theology. Kendrick's Creek, Tenn.

WILLIAM JEFFERSON BAKER, '86 law. Practicing law at Cuero, Tex.

ROBERT ALEXANDER CODY, '86 theology. Editor *Student*. Withe, Tenn.

WILLIAM TAYLOR WATSON, '86 law. Weatherford, Tex.

HALLETT HARDING, '87. Fort Worth, Tex.

JAMES WALTER BRANNUM, '86 law. N. E. corner Eighth and Main streets, Kansas City, Mo.

HARRY MANEY DRIPOOS, '86 law. Nashville, Tenn.

WILLIAM HAWES EPPS, '86 law. Hawes Cross Roads, Tenn.

ROBERT BONE WILLIAMS, '87. Delegate from Amasagassean Society to Tennessee inter-collegiate oratorical contest. Henderson's Cross Roads, Tenn.

NATHAN WALLER, '89. Selma, Ala.

ORVILLE TRUMAN STONE, '87. Tremont, Miss.

## XLVIII.

WILLIAM HENRY MARTIN, '87 law. Las Casas, Tenn.

EDWARD EVERETT SNEED, '87 law. Milton, Tenn.

JUNIUS WILDIN BECK, '87. Smithysgrove, Ky.

GEORGE BECKER KILPATRICK, Lebanon, Tenn.

JOHN HOWELL NOBLE, Anniston, Ala.

## DENISON CHAPTER.

### [The Alpha Eta, at Denison University, Granville, O.]

Denison University, founded in 1831, is the only Baptist college in Ohio. It comprises a college department and a preparatory department. In the college there are eleven instructors and about eighty students. Degrees are given in arts, philosophy, and science; but the classical course of prescribed studies are still the favorite. Women are not admitted.

The fraternities are Sigma Chi, Beta Theta Pi, and Phi Gamma Delta. The average membership is ten. Preparatory students are not initiated.

The Alpha Eta was founded in 1868 and has contributed many energetic workers to Beta Theta Pi. Chas. J. Seaman, of this chapter, was for several years the agent and editor of the song book and was the editor of the catalogue of 1881. He was also the chief founder of the Wooglin club house on Chantauqua Lake. Chas. H. Carey was chief of the district in 1881-'82. W. C. Sprague was an editor of the magazine in 1882-'83 and 1885-'86. F. W. Shepardson has been an editor of the magazine from 1883 to the present time. He has published a history of the chapter. The recent corresponding secretaries have been F. W. Shepardson, W. C. Sheppard, Will B. Owen, and E. H. Castle. At conventions there have been the following representatives: 1881, W. C. Sprague and J. J. Robinson; 1882, F. W. Shepardson, W. C. Shepard, F. M. Stalker, W. C. Sprague, H. L. Jones, and G. Ellison, the first of whom was secretary; 1883, C. J. Seaman.

**Admitted since August, 1881.**

### XLIII.

WILLIAM COLLINS SHEPPARD, '84. Captain of Denison Cadets; editor *Collegian, Adytum, Commencement Daily;* cor. sec.; graduated A. B. from University of Rochester; principal Hanover, Ohio, public schools, 1883-4; principal Johnstown public schools, 1885-6. Present address, Johnstown, Ohio; permanent address, Bucyrus, Ohio.

GARRETT ELLISON, '85. No. 9 East Ninth street, Kansas City, Mo.

### XLIV.

HERBERT LYON JONES, '86. Publisher *Collegian;* debater Franklin Society Annual. Granville, Ohio.

CHARLES SILVEY SPRAGUE, '86. Cor. sec.; orator preliminary contest, '84; secretary D. U. Oratorical Association, 1884-5; captain Gymnasium Association, '85; editor *Collegian* and *Denison Weekly News;* president Reading Room and Lecture Association; on Franklin Annual, '84. McConnellsville, O.

CHARLES WOOD EBERLEIN, '86. McConnellsville, O.

DAVID WILBUR BROWNELL, '86. Five prizes field day, 1883; debater Franklin Annual; now studying law. Permanent address, McConnellsville, Ohio; present address, 25 German American Bank Block, St. Paul, Minn.

### XLV.

ELMER ELLSWORTH KITCHEN, '86. Debater Franklin commencement, '83. Attending University of Denver, Denver, Col.

JOHN LUTHER WILKIN, '86. Read the "Chronicles" at class reception, 1883. Toledo, O.

CHARLES GRANT RANK, '86. "Address of Welcome" freshman reception, 1883. Ticket agent of B. & O. R. R. at Newark, O.

WILLIAM BISHOP OWEN, '87. Orator Franklin commencement, '85; editor *Collegian:* cor, sec. Granville, O.

HENRY DWIGHT HERVEY, '88. Granville, O.

BURTON BANKS TUTTLE. Prize essay; city editor Brantford daily paper. Brantford, Ont.

DANIEL SHEPARDSON, JR., '88. Debater Franklin Extra, '84. Address, Granville, Licking county. O.

### XLVI.

HENRY MARTYN CARTER, '86. Assistant in chemical laboratory; now at Boston School of Technology. Present address, 295 Columbus avenue, Boston, Mass.; home address, Granville, O.

EDWARD HOWARD CASTLE, '88. Debater Franklin Extra, '84. Cor. sec. Alexandria, O.

WILLIAM CLEMENT SHAFER, '88. Declaimer Franklin Extra, '84. Present address, Kingwood, W. Va.; permanent address, Parkersburg, W. Va.

HOWARD COPLAND, '88. Now at University of Montana, Deer Lodge, Montana.

### XLVII.

GORMAN JONES, '89. West Jefferson, O.

WILLIAM HENRY DAVIES, '89. North-east corner Sixth and Harrison, Topeka, Kas.

WILLIAM ERNEST CASTLE, '89. Alexandria, O.

EVAN G. EVANS, '89. "Crescent" Franklin Extra, '85. Granville, O.

RALPH PARSONS SMITH, '88. Poet Franklin commencement, '85. Granville, O.

HARRY JAY KENDIG, '86. Second at oratorical contest, 1886. Hayesville, O.

EDMUND A. WILLIAMS, '89. Debater Franklin Extra, '85. Granville, O.

JAMES STANLEY BROWN, '89. Declaimer Calliopean Extra, '85. High Hill, O.

# DE PAUW CHAPTER.

### (The Delta, at De Pauw University, Greencastle, Ind.)

De Pauw University was founded in 1837, and until 1884 was known as Indiana Asbury University. Schools of theology, law, music, fine arts, pedagogics, military science, and horticulture have recently been established. The university was recently endowed by W. C. De Pauw, and $84.000 have been expended on grounds, buildings, and apparatus. The college department has four courses of study and is called the Asbury college of liberal arts. The college has thirteen instructors and about two hundred and fifty students. There is also a preparatory department. Women are admitted to all departments. Tuition is practically free. The aggregate number of students in all departments is six hundred and eighty.

The fraternities are Beta Theta Pi, Phi Gamma Delta, Sigma Chi, Phi Kappa Psi, Delta Kappa Epsilon, Phi Delta Theta, and Delta Tau Delta. The membership varies from fifteen to twenty-five. Excepting Beta Theta Pi and Delta Kappa Epsilon, all of the fraternities initiate preparatory students. The fraternities are addicted to combinations.

The Delta was founded in 1845 and has always been one of our principal chapters. Edwin H. Terrell, of this chapter, was one of the editors of the catalogue of 1881 and was also one of the founders of the Wooglin club. He was president of the convention of 1884. Frank M. Joyce has for several years been the business manager of the fraternity magazine; and E. L. Martin was one of the business managers 1883-'84. A. N. Grant was chief of the district in 1881-'82 and 1882-'83, and J. G. Campbell was chief in 1885-'86. The recent corresponding secretaries have been W. Iglehart, C. W. Bennett, J. G. Campbell, and M. E. Hector. The representatives at recent conventions were, in 1881, F. M. Joyce, C. S. Olcott, and Will Iglehart; in 1882, C. L. Urmston, G. B. Moore, E. L. Martin; in 1883 Worth Merritt; in 1884, J. E. Durham and E. H. Terrell; in 1885, J. G. Campbell, F. M. Joyce, and Will Iglehart.

Iota. Salem, Ind.; temporary address, Greencastle, Ind.

ALGIE PERRY GULICK, '87. Second lieutenant in cadet corps; trustee of Platonian Literary Society. Rantoul, Ill.

JOHN PHILLIPS REASONER, '88. Instructor in takigraphy, '84; now teaching; will be in college next year. Cerro Gordo, Ill.

WILLIAM SAMUEL SCOTT, '88. Left college in 1884. Greencastle, Ind.

HOWARD McELROY, '87. Teaching at Alvin, Ill. Permanent address, Rossville, Ill.

JOHN HELPS BICKFORD, '88. Niles, Mich.

GEORGE HOWARD MURPHY, '88. Second sergeant in cadet corps; class historian. Permanent address, Greencastle, Ind.

### XLVII.

WILLIAM LINCOLN HESTER, '87. Initiated at Pi. New Albany, Ind.

HARRY BOWSER, '88. Second lieutenant and ranking man of his class in the cadet corps. Indianapolis, Ind.

JOHN LEE BENEDICT, '87. Second lieutenant in cadet corps. Rantoul, Ill.

CHARLES POST BENEDICT, '89. First sergeant and ranking man of his class in cadet corps. Rantoul, Ill.

ISAAC JARVIS HAMMOND, '89. Greencastle, Ind.

JOHN FREDERICK CLEARWATERS, '89. Thorntown, Ind.

### XLVIII.

FRANK PERRY IRVIN, '86. Initiated at Theta. Piqua, O.

FRANK THEODORE PENNINGTON, '86. Initiated at Theta. Tiffin, O.

SQUIRE ROBINSON GREER, '86. Initiated at Theta. Oxford, O.

### DICKINSON CHAPTER.

[The Alpha Sigma, at Dickinson College, Carlisle, Pa.]

Dickinson was founded in 1783. It was originally a Presbyterian institution, but long ago it passed into the hands of the Methodist Episcopal church. Women have recently been admitted, In the college department there are eight professors and about one hundred students. There is also a preparatory school.

The fraternities are Phi Kappa Psi, Sigma Chi, Theta Delta Chi, Chi Phi, Beta Theta Pi, and Phi Delta Theta. Membership varies from six to twenty.

The Alpha Sigma has had an excellent record ever since its founding in 1874; but this sketch can not go back farther than four or five years. In 1881–'82 it had a junior contest medal and an editor of the college paper; in 1882–'83, first honor and valedictory, third honor, class historian, and also the first freshman honor; in 1883–'84, first honor in the junior class and also in the sophomore class, and two editors of the college paper; 1884–'85, second honor and salutatory, freshman prize in English, and an editor of the college paper. In 1881, and again in 1882, the chapter published a college annual, the *Minutal*. The chapter usually numbers only about eight men. It does not admit preparatory students until after they have passed their entrance examination. The recent corresponding secretaries have been L. T. Appold, F. G. Graham, F. T. Baker, and F. M. Welsh. Baker was chief of the district in 1884–'85, and Welsh in 1885–'86.

Admitted since August, 1881.

#### XLIII.

DAVID BROWN, '85. Editor *Dickinsonian;* anniversarian Union Philosophical Society; on base-ball nine. Philadelphia, Pa.

FRANK GORDON GRAHAM, A. B. '83. Third honor; editor *Dickinsonian;* on base-ball nine; with *Kansas City Times*. Kansas City, Mo.

GEORGE FRANCIS PETTINOS, '85. At Lehigh University; editor *Lehigh Annual*. Permanent address, Carlisle, Pa.; temporary address, Bethlehem, Pa.

ELBERT WILLIAMS OSBORN, '85. Niagara Falls, N. Y.

#### XLIV.

JOHN ULMSTEAD DETRICK, '85. On foot-ball and base-ball teams. 108 S. Charles street, Baltimore, Md.

JOHN FRANKLIN REIGART, '86. Led freshman and sophomore classes; teaching. North Hope, Pa.

FRANK THOMAS BAKER, A. B. '85. Salutatorian and second honor; editor *Dickinsonian;* on base-ball nine; cor. sec.; chief district III.; teaching. Mount Holly. N. Y.

#### XLV.

CHARLES EARL BIKLE, '86. Third in junior class; on base-ball nine. Hagerstown, Md.

WILLARD GEOFFREY LAKE, '87. Editor *College Annual;* captain of foot-ball eleven; on base-ball nine; conductor of Philharmonic Society. Seabright, N. J.

#### XLVI.

FRANKLIN MOORE WELSH, '88. Freshman prize in English; cor. sec ; chief district III. Philadelphia, Pa.

LEWIS ADAMS PARSELS, '89. On foot-ball eleven. South Dennis, N. J.

GERALD WOOD CRANE SMOOT. Tompkinsville, Charles county, Md.

WILLIAM BLAIR STEWART, '87. Editor of *College Annual,* but resigned. Newville, Pa.

JOSEPH CASTLE REYNOLDS, '88. Class historian. 1127 Green street, Philadelphia, Pa.

#### XLVII.

ALBERT E. MEILY, '89. Harrisburg, Pa.

JOHN ROBINSON TODD, '87. Graduate of Drew Theological Seminary; editor *College Annual*. Snow Hill, Md.

#### XLVIII.

ALBERT DUNCAN YOCUM, '89. Everett, Pa.

## HAMPDEN SIDNEY CHAPTER.

### (The Zeta, at Hampden Sidney College, Hampden Sidney College P. O., Va.)

The college is a Presbyterian institution that was established in 1776. There are seven professors and about one hundred and twenty-five students. Almost all of the students take the classical course of prescribed studies. Women are not admitted. A theological school and a preparatory school are in the immediate neighborhood and are managed in sympathy with the college.

Beta Theta Pi, Phi Kappa Psi, Chi Phi, Phi Gamma Delta, Sigma Chi, and Kappa Sigma are the fraternities, with an average membership of twelve.

The Zeta was founded in 1850 and is our oldest chapter in Virginia. The recent corresponding secretaries have been A. D. Drew, W. D. Spurlin, C. L. Stribling, W. M. Hollady, J. D. Eggleston, Jr., H. C. V. Campbell, and W. A. Watson. W. C. White, of Zeta, was chief of the district in 1882-'83. At the convention of 1881 the chapter was represented by G. J. Ramsay; at that of 1882, by W. C. White; and at that of 1884, by C. C. Lewis, H. C. V. Campbell, and A. C. Finley.

**Admitted since August, 1881.**

#### XLIII.

CHARLES RIDDLE STRIBLING, A. B., '84. Martinsburg, W. Va.

WILLIS HENRY BOBOCK, A. B., '84. Sophomore medal of Phip. Society; divided first honor, 1884; University of Virginia, 1884-'85. Hampden Sidney College, Va.

#### XLIV.

JOSEPH DUPUY EGGLESTON, JR, '86. Cor. sec.; delivered senior medal, 1886. Hampden Sidney College, Va.

JOHN BOOKER FINLEY, '84. Senior medalist of Phip. Society; editor of *Hampden Sidney Magazine*; teaching. Present address, Mossy Creek, Va.; permanent address, Romney, W. Va.

#### XLV.

WILLIAM BRODNAX HOPKINS, '86. Charlestown, Jefferson county, W. Va.

ROBERT EDWARD LEE BLANTON, '86. Senior orator of Union Society. Farmville, Va.

CHARLES CAMERON LEWIS, JR., '87. Charleston, Kanawha county, W. Va.

HENRY CLAY VAN METRE CAMPBELL, '86. Elected editor-in-chief of *Hampden Sidney Magazine* in 1885; cor. sec.; chief. Gerardstown, W. Va.

HENRY READ McILWAINE, A. B., '85. Editor-in-chief of *Hampden Sidney Magazine*, 1884-'85; teaching at Lewisburg, W. Va. Permanent address, Petersburg, Pa.

#### XLVI.

THOMAS THWEATT JONES, '87. San Marino, Va.

HUGH AUGUSTUS WHITE, '86. Editor and manager *Magazine* in 1885, and business manager in 1886; commencement orator Phip. Society 1885; senior orator. 1886. Moorefield. W. Va.

WILLIAM HENRY WILSON, '87. Editor and manager *Magazine* in 1886; commencement orator Phip. Society, 1886. Hampden Sidney College, Va.

DANIEL SEPTIMUS EVANS, JR., '88. Concord Depot, Va.

ROBERT ASHLIN WHITE, '87. Moorefield. W. Va.

CHARLES HOWES HAMMOND, '88. 384 N. Charles St., Baltimore, Md.

ABNER CRUMP HOPKINS, JR., '87. Charlestown, Jefferson county, W. Va.

WALTER ALLEN WATSON, '87. Editor and manager *Magazine* in 1885; commencement orator Phip. Society, 1886; cor. sec. Jennings' Ordinary, Nottoway county, Va.

JAMES MAXWELL STRIBLING, '88. Martinsburg, W. Va.

#### XLVII.

JAMES POAGUE EPES, '88. Blackstone, Va.

ANGUS ROBERTSON SHAW. Student in the Union Theological Seminary. Hampden Sidney College, Va.

## HANOVER CHAPTER.

[The Iota, at Hanover College, Hanover, Ind.]

Hanover was founded in 1833 and is controlled by the Presbyterians. Women are admitted. In the college department there are six professors and about ninety students. There is also a preparatory department.

The fraternities are Beta Theta Pi, Phi Gamma Delta, Phi Delta Theta, Sigma Chi, Delta Tau Delta. A chapter commonly numbers about ten members.

The Iota dates from 1853. The recent corresponding secretaries have been R. E. Schuh, G. W. Wyatt. G. W. Giboney. D. C. Blyth, J. W. Robbins, and J. E. Abrams. Robbins was chief of the district in 1884-'85. At the convention of 1881 the representatives were E. E. Silliman, L. J. Duncan, and Rev. E. J. Brown; and at that of 1882, Rev. E. J. Brown, J. B. Tucker, and R. E. Schuh.

### Admitted since August, 1881.

#### XLIII.

James Bently Tucker, '85. Now at De Pauw University. Home, Salem, Ind.

Virgil Emmet Tucker, '86. Insurance agent. Omaha, Neb.

Smith O'Neal, '86. Teacher. Permanent address, Carrollton, Ky.

Rev. William Bell Riley, A. B. '85. Associate editor *Hanover Monthly;* pastor Baptist churches at Warsaw and Carrollton, Ky., since June, '85; now student at Baptist Theological Seminary, Louisville, Ky. Present address, Waverly Hotel, Louisville. Ky.

#### XLV.

Thomas Reed Bridges, '87. Carrollton, Ky.

#### XLVI.

James Elva Abrams, '87. Moscow, O.

Richard Francis Evans, '86. Laconia, Ind.

Orlando Bronson Riley, '87. Student Baptist Theological Seminary, Louisville, Ky., 1884-'85. New Liberty, Ky.

Oscar Snyder Wilson, '88. Swanville, Ind.

Winfield Scott Smith, '88. Vincennes, Ind.

Junius Coston Clemmons, '88. Hanover, Ind.

#### XLVII.

John Wesley Rowlett, '89. Bedford, Ky.

Robert Matthew Dillon, '89. Madison, Ind.

Walter Levi Riley, '89. New Liberty, Ky.

# HARVARD CHAPTER.

(The Eta, at Harvard University, Cambridge, Mass.)

Harvard University comprises the college, the scientific school, the divinity school, the law school, the medical school, the dental school, the school of agriculture and horticulture, several museums and laboratories, the observatory, the library, and the graduate department. The total number of instructors is about two hundred. In the college there are about one thousand students, all candidates for A. B. There are usually five or six hundred students in the other departments. In the college the course after freshman year is wholly elective, and the practice of the more careful students is to devote their last two years almost wholly to some special line of study. There are good opportunities for advanced work in almost any branch: for example, each of the following subjects has from ten to twenty electives—Greek, Latin, French, German, Philosophy, History, Mathematics, Physics, Chemistry, and Natural History; and besides there are courses in many other subjects. In all departments of the university text-books are used comparatively little, and great stress is laid upon original research.

There are chapters of Alpha Delta Phi, Beta Theta Pi, Zeta Psi, Theta Delta Chi, and Delta Upsilon. These are named in the order of original foundation; but no one of them has had a continuous existence. Many of the members of the fraternities are also members of a sophomore club familiarly called the Dickey, which many years ago was a chapter of Delta Kappa Epsilon.

The Eta was founded in 1843 and was revived in 1880. The recent corresponding secretaries have been H. W. Winkley, E. L. Underwood, W. M. McInnes, M. W. Fredrick, A. R. Baum, and Walter Alexander. McInnes was chief of the district in 1883-'84. The representatives at the convention of 1881 were Eugene Wambaugh and Chambers Baird, Jr.; at that of 1882, the same; at that of 1883. A. de R. McNair, E. Wambaugh, Howard Lilienthal, and H. W. Winkley; at that of 1884, E. Wambaugh and C. Baird, Jr.; and at that of 1885, C. Baird, Jr. Baird and Wambaugh have been editors of the BETA THETA PI, and the latter was general secretary from 1881 to 1884. Hon. Peleg Emory Aldrich, one of the founders, is a member of the board of directors.

### Admitted since August, 1881.

#### XLIII.

WILLIAM HALL WILLIAMS, '83. Melrose, Mass.

#### XLIV.

WILLIAM MORROW McINNES, '85. Cor. sec. and chief. 1 Akron street, Boston, Mass.

BARTOW BEE RAMAGE, '84. Came from Alpha Chi. Newberry, S. C.

#### XLV.

FREDERIC CLARK HOOD, '86. 31 Crescent avenue, Chelsea, Mass.

EDWARD STAPLES DROWN, '84. Newburyport, Mass.

JULIAN CLIFFORD JAYNES, '84 theo. Admitted at Alpha Pi. West Newton, Mass.

NATHAN CUSHMAN STEVENS, '83. Admitted at Beta. Willoughby, O.

RALPH DENTON WILSON, '83. 2 Divinity avenue, Cambridge, Mass.

MARCUS WHITE FREDRICK, '84. Member of Pierian Sodality; cor. sec. Virginia City, Nev.

JOHN BENSON JENKINS, '85 law. From Alpha Kappa and Omicron. Norfolk, Va.

#### XLVI.

GILBERT NORRIS JONES, '84. Phi Beta Kappa. Bangor, Me.

EDWARD EVERETT BLODGETT, '87. 397 Beacon street, Boston, Mass.

ALEXANDER ROBERT BAUM, '87. Cor. sec. 1705 Powell street, San Francisco, Cal.

WALTER ALEXANDER, '87. Cor. sec. St Charles, Mo.

HERBERT TUFTS ALLEN, '86. Catcher university base-ball nine. Corner Boston and Washington streets, Somerville, Mass.

EDWIN JOSEPH MEEKS, '87. 50 East Eighty-third street, New York, N. Y.

ALFRED GAITHER, '87. Special. 131 Broadway, Cincinnati, O.

HENRY C. HOLT, '86. Winchester, Mass.

H. W. MAGILL, '86. Cincinnati, O.

CLINTON COLLINS, '86. Cincinnati, O.

P. S. HOWE, '86. Brookline, Mass.

W. A. BROOKS, '87. Haverhill, Mass.

F. M. TILDEN, '87. Chicago, Ill.

WAKEFIELD BAKER, '87. San Francisco, Cal.

## INDIANA UNIVERSITY CHAPTER.

### The Pi, at Indiana University, Bloomington Ind.

The Indiana University belongs to the state. In the college department there are usually about one hundred and sixty students. Degrees are conferred in arts, letters, philosophy, and science. During the latter half of the course the studies are largely elective. There are eighteen instructors. Besides the college, there is a preparatory department, with about one hundred students. Women are admitted to both departments.

Beta Theta Pi, Phi Delta Theta, Sigma Chi, Phi Kappa Psi, and Phi Gamma Delta are the fraternities. Preparatory students are admitted. Chapters average seventeen members. The various fraternities and the non-fraternity men are constantly forming combinations.

Since the convention of 1881 the corresponding secretaries of the Pi have been G. W. Cromer, A. D. Moffet, A. C. Patton, N. L. Bunnell, and F. W. Walters. F. C. Davis, O. P. Erskine, and J. L. Mackey were the representatives at the convention of 1881; A. D. Moffet at that of 1882; and A. C. Patton at those of 1883 and 1884. The chapter is usually much smaller than its rivals, seldom exceeding twelve members. It was founded in 1845.

#### Admitted since August, 1881.

#### XLIII.

FRANK HOWARD HUGHES, '85. Bloomington, Ind.

MELVILLE GRESHARDT ESHMAN, '84. Los Angeles, Cal.

HERMAN CARR, '85. Columbus, Ind.

ELMER ELSWORTH MULLINIX, '85. Cloverdale, Ind.

CLARENCE MILTON PARKS, '85. Studying medicine at Cincinnati. Sullivan, Ind.

ORRIS EVERETT MULLINIX, '88. Cloverdale, Ind.

WADE HAMPTON GALLOWAY, '86. Gosport, Ind.

#### XLIV.

JOSEPH WRIGHT WHARTON, 965 North Mississippi street, Indianapolis, Ind.

ADAM CARL PATTON, '84. Law student. Greeley, Col.

MORTON LAUGE GOULD, '84. 426 North Fifth street, Terre Haute, Ind.

VIRGIL E. TUCKER, '86. New Philadelphia, Ind.

ALBERT RABB, '87. Second on civil service contest; captain and catcher of college ball nine; president of Oratorical Association and business manager of *Student*. Snoddy's Mills, Ind.

HOWARD D. MAXWELL, '86. Now at Wabash College. Rockville, Ind.

#### XLV.

WILLIAM LINCOLN HESTER, '87. Now at De Pauw. New Albany, Ind.

CHARLES HENRY OLER, '87. Economy, Ind.

NEWTON LOMER BUNNELL, '87. Teaching. Green's Fork, Ind.

#### XLVI.

HOMER LEONARD, '87. Smithville, Ind.

FRANCIS MARION WALTERS, '87. Greensburg, Ind.

ALBERT MILLER, '88. Bloomington, Ind.

ROBERT FOSTER HIGHT, '88. Bloomington, Ind.

WALTER DUNN HOWE, '90. Ft. Snelling, Minn.

JOSEPH FRANCIS THORNTON, '88. Associate editor of *Student*, Bedford, Ind.

CHARLES MORTON CUNNINGHAM, '88. Greensburg, Ind.

BEDFORD VANCE SUDBURY, '89. Bloomington, Ind.

#### XLVII.

CHARLES ROLLAND MADISON, '90. Bloomington, Ind.

DANIEL W. CROCKETT, '89. Sudbury, Ind.

JOHN SINGLETON SHANNON, '88. Greensburg, Decatur county, Ind.

HARRY EDMUND WISE, '88. 1409 Leavenworth street, San Francisco, Cal.

WALTER WYVTE, '90. Cutler, Ind.

JOSEPH HENRY HOWARD, '88. Came from Butler; charter member of Alpha Psi; second prize on temperance contest. 308 North Ash street, Indianapolis, Ind.

CHAS. S. THOMAS, Pendleton, Ind.

JOHN DETWILER ATKINSON, Pennsville, Pa.

## UNIVERSITY OF IOWA CHAPTER.

### [The Alpha Beta, at the University of Iowa, Iowa City, Ia.]

In the college department of the University of Iowa there are about two hundred and fifty students, and in the law and medical schools there are about three hundred and fifty. There is no preparatory department.

Beta Theta Pi, Phi Kappa Psi, Delta Tau Delta, Phi Delta Theta, and Sigma Chi are represented.

The membership of the Alpha Beta varies from twelve to twenty. The chapter was founded in 1866. The recent corresponding secretaries have been H. W. Seaman, W. N. Baker, H. P. Mozier, R. C. Lake, W. F. Mozier, and E. H. Sabin. H. P. Mozier was chief of the district in 1883-'84. T. G. Newman attended the convention of 1881; J. I. Gilbert that of 1882; R. C. Lake and M. H. Dey that of 1884; and C. M. Porter that of 1885. W. B. Burnet of this chapter is a member of the board of directors.

### Admitted since August, 1881.

#### XLIII.

ELBERT LELAND JOHNSON, '84. Member of Lambda. Clay Centre, Kans.

DONALD D. DONNAN, '85. Divided sophomore elocution prize '82; declaimer on Irving exhibition '83; secretary state senate '86; editor *Elkader Journal.*. Elkader, Ia.

HARRY DOUGLAS ALLEN, '85. Waterloo, Ia.

SAMUEL PARKER GILBERT, '84. Burlington, Ia.

#### XLIV.

HARRY PRESTON MOZIER, '84. Declaimer on Zet. exhibition '82; one of commencement speakers. Permanent address. Iowa City, Ia.; present address, 1528 Q street N. W., Washington, D. C.

FRANK ORRIN LOWDEN, '85. Debater on Zet. exhibition '83 and '85; valedictorian. Burlington, Ia.

CHARLES MORSEMAN PORTER, '86. Iowa City, Ia.

ALLEN SHELBURN BURROWS, '86. Norfolk, Neb.

NORMAN MADISON CAMPBELL, '86. Sophomore elocution prize '83; Irving exhibition debater '85; Irving June orator '85; on *Vidette Reporter* '83-'85. Colorado Springs, Col.

WILLIAM SUMNER HARWOOD. On *Chicago Inter-Ocean.* 29 Hermitage avenue, Chicago, Ill.; former address, Charles City, Ia.

WILLIAM FOY MOZIER, '86. On *Vidette Reporter.* Iowa City, Ia.

#### XLV.

WILLIAM MORSE WOODWARD, '86. Elocution prize '82; Irving exhibition declaimer '84; captain foot-ball team. Independence, Ia.

ELBRIDGE H. SABIN, '86. Clinton, Ia.

MARVIN HULL DEY, '87. Iowa City, Ia.

#### XLVI.

ELWYN FRANK BROWN, '87. Irving exhibition debater '86. Jefferson, Ia.

RICHARD DREW MUSSER, '88. Muscatine, Ia.

DAVID POWELL JOHNSON, JR., '88. Muscatine, Ia.

EDWARD MOSES NEALLEY, '87. In business at Burlington, Ia.

#### XLVII.

BROD BEDFORD DAVIS, '89. Lewis, Ia.

JOHN HOWARD GATES, '88. Waterloo, Ia.

FRED S. WATKINS, '88. Davenport, Ia.

GEORGE SPENCER WRIGHT, '89. Council Bluffs, Ia.

#### XLVIII.

FRANK PRENTICE WRIGHT, '89. Council Bluffs, Ia.

GEORGE WILLIAM INGHAM, '89. Algona, Ia.

WALTER LINCOLN ANDERSON, '89. Sidney, Ia.

GEORGE WASHINGTON SWIGART. Maquoketa, Ia.

## IOWA WESLEYAN CHAPTER.

### [The Alpha Epsilon, at Iowa Wesleyan University, Mt. Pleasant, Ia.]

The college department of the Iowa Wesleyan University has twelve instructors and about one hundred and twenty-five students. There are about one hundred and seventy-five students in the preparatory department and the conservatory of music. Women are admitted.

The fraternities are Beta Theta Pi and Phi Delta Theta. There is a strong anti-fraternity sentiment, fostered by the president.

The Alpha Epsilon was founded in 1868. It usually numbers about ten members. Since the convention of 1881. G. W. Latham, Edson Gregg, G. S. Williams, and W. B. Hanna have been corresponding secretaries. Hanna represented the chapter at the convention of 1885.

### Admitted since August, 1881.

#### XLIII.

WILL LEWIS COLLINS, '84. In Knoxville National Bank, Knoxville, Ia.

GEORGE ANDREW HARE, '84. Now in medical department of University of Michigan. Permanent address, Mt. Pleasant, Ia.

CARL SCHURZ WILLIAMS, '84. Represented the students on University Day, '84; cor. sec. Now at Belleville, Kan.; permanent address, Centreville, Ia.

#### XLIV.

ASBURY NELSON LOPER, '84. Teaching in Newton, Kan. Permanent address, Sperry, Ia.

JOHN WAUGH LANEY, '86. Rosendale, Mo.

HOWARD THOMAS PASCHAL, '86. Studying law at Creston, Ia.

CLYDE PLEASANTON PASCHAL, '86. Studying law in Creston, Ia.

#### XLV.

WALTER TEIS SMITH, '86. At University of

Michigan. Member of Lambda, Pepin, Ill.

WILLIAM BLAKEWAY HANNA, '87. Assistant in chemical laboratory, '82-'83 and '85-'86; cor. sec. Danville, Ia.

#### XLVI.

JAMES LEIGH WOOLSON, '87. Local editor *Iowa Wesleyan*, '85-'86. Mt. Pleasant, Ia.

FREDERIC LINCOLN TOENNIGS, '88. Pepin, Ill.

BYRON LAMONT CLOSE GANN, '89. Maryville, Mo.

JOSEPH HOUSEMAN NEWBOLD, '89. Mt. Pleasant, Ia.

#### XLVII.

OWEN GREGG WILSON, '89. Washington, Ia.

CHARLES ROBERT WOODEN, '89. Centreville, Ia.

PAUL BIRD WOOLSON, '88. Mt. Pleasant, Ia.

ERNEST FREDERICK SMITH, '89. Pepin, Ill.

OTTO HENRY UNLAND, '89. Pepin, Ill.

## JOHNS HOPKINS CHAPTER.

[The Alpha Chi, at Johns Hopkins University, Baltimore, Md.]

The Johns Hopkins University is best known because of the prominence that it gives to post-graduate study. Yet there are also undergraduates. There are usually about one hundred and seventy-five post-graduates, one hundred undergraduates, and forty or fifty special students. There are forty-three instructors. The institution is only ten years old; and its almost immediate advance to the front rank was due to its great wealth and intelligent management.

The only fraternities are Beta Theta Pi, Phi Kappa Psi, and Delta Phi. As the university is situated in the heart of the city and has no dormitories, the students are very much scattered. Besides, each one is pursuing a specialty and so meets only the few who are studying in the same line. The fraternities are encouraged by the authorities as furnishing the best means of overcoming these difficulties and of promoting acquaintance among the students.

Since the convention of 1881 the corresponding secretaries of the Alpha Chi have been Edgar Goodman, W. S. Bayley, J. P. Campbell, and A. R. L. Dohme. The chapter was founded in 1878. It was represented in 1881 and in 1884 by S. G. Boyle; and in 1885 by Lee Sale.

### Admitted since August, 1881.

#### XLIII.

LOUIS GARTHE, '82. Reporter for the *Baltimore Sun*. Baltimore, Md.

JOHN DEERING LORD, JR., '84. On ball nine; now studying law at Columbia and member of Alpha Alpha. Baltimore, Md.

WILLIAM SHIRLEY BAYLEY, '83. Assistant in mineralogy '82; assistant in chemistry '83; holder of fellowship in chemistry, '84-'85, and in geology '85-'86; cor. sec.; now studying mineralogy at the Johns Hopkins University. 366 North avenue W., Baltimore, Md.

ARTHUR THOMAS COLLINS, '83. Assistant in chemistry '85. Mt. Washington, Md.

#### XLIV.

WILLIAM BEATTY HARLAN, '83. Attorney at law. Baltimore, Md.; residence, Churchville, Md.

HENRY WINSLOW WILLIAMS, '83. LL. B., University of Maryland, '85; attorney at law. Baltimore, Md.

DE WITT B. BRACE. Admitted at Upsilon; A. B., Boston University, '81. Boston, Mass.

FREDERICK SCHILLER LEE, Ph. D. '84. Graduate scholarship in biology '83, and fellowship; admitted at Beta Zeta; A. B., St. Lawrence University, '78; now studying in Europe. Fort Plain, N. Y.

HENRY HAZLEHURST WIEGAND, '85. Still at Johns Hopkins University. 272 Madison avenue, Baltimore, Md.

MAURICE FELS, '83. LL. B., University of Pennsylvania, '85; attorney at law. Philadelphia, Pa.

JOHN PENDLETON CAMPBELL, '85. Cor. sec.; graduate scholarship '85-'86. Permanent address, Charlestown, W. Va.; temporary address, 352 N. Eutaw street, Baltimore, Md.

#### XLV.

MANSFIELD THEODORE PEED. A. M., Randolph Macon, '78, and member of Alpha Xi. Petersburg, Va.

HERBERT CHARLES ELMER. Member of Beta Delta. Home, Rushford, N. Y.; temporary address, 93 W. Preston street, Baltimore, Md.

THEODORE HOUGH, '86. Hopkins honorary scholarship '84-'86. 181 McCulloh street, Baltimore, Md.

#### XLVI.

EVERT B. SMEDES. A. B., University of North Carolina, '83; teaching. Raleigh, N. C.

ALFRED ROBERT LOUIS DOHME, '86. Cor. sec.; on ball nine; vice-president '86. 27 Hollins street, Baltimore, Md.

JOHN RANDOLPH WINSLOW, '86. 23 McCulloh street, Baltimore, Md.

JAMES CLARK FIFIELD, '87. Permanent address, Kearney, Neb.; temporary, 182 N. Eutaw street, Baltimore, Md.

WILLIAM FLOOD SMITH, '86. Hopkins honorary scholarship '84-'86. 45 Harlem avenue, Baltimore, Md.

ALFRED DODGE COLE. Appointed professor of chemistry and physics at Denison University '85; came from Kappa. Permanent address, Beverly, Mass.; present address, Granville, O.

JAMES LEE LOVE. A. B., University of North Carolina, '84. Appointed assistant professor of mathematics at University of North Carolina '85. Permanent address, Gastonia, N. C.

#### XLVII.

HENRY R. SLACK, JR. Graduated at Maryland College of Pharmacy in '85; received three prizes from Georgia Pharmacy Association; now in business. La Grange, Ga.

JOHN WHITE, JR., '88. Permanent address, Poolesville, Md.; temporary address, 258 Linden avenue, Baltimore, Md.

JAMES HIGGINS McINTOSH. A. B., Newberry College, '84. Home address, Newberry, S. C.; temporary address, 333 N. Eutaw street, Baltimore, Md.

JOSEPH HOEING KASTLE. A. B., Kentucky University, '84; graduate scholarship in chemistry '85-'86. Permanent address, Lexington, Ky.; temporary address, 333 N. Eutaw street, Baltimore, Md.

CHARLES EDWARD SIMON, '88. Hopkins scholarship '85. 201 Linden avenue, Baltimore, Md.

WILLIAM HOWARD MILLER, '88. Hopkins honorary scholarship '85-'88. 141 E. Townsend street, Baltimore, Md.

FREDERICK GEORGE YOUNG, '86. Home, Beaver Dam, Wis ; temporary address, 87 W. Preston street, Baltimore, Md.

GEORGE MURRAY CAMPBELL, A. B., Dlahousie University, '82. Home, Truro, N. S.; temporary address, 185 Linden avenue, Baltimore, Md.

THOMAS SPEAR FEARN, '88. Home, Summit, N. J.; temporary address, 132 W. Madison street, Baltimore, Md.

EDWARD CAREY APPLEGARTH, '87. Hopkins honorary scholarship '84-'87. 632 W. Fayette street, Baltimore, Md.

### UNIVERSITY OF KANSAS CHAPTER.

#### [The Alpha Nu, at the University of Kansas, Lawrence, Kas.]

In the college department of the University of Kansas there are about two hundred students, one-third being women. Degrees are conferred in arts and in science. There is great freedom in choice of studies after the sophomore year. There are also normal, law, pharmacy, music, and preparatory departments. The institution is under the management of a board of regents appointed by the governor of the state, and receives its financial support from the sale of university lands and from appropriations made by the legislature.

The fraternities represented in the order of their founding are Beta Theta Pi, Phi Kappa Psi, Phi Gamma Delta, Phi Delta Theta, Sigma Chi, and Sigma Nu.

The Alpha Nu was represented in the convention of '81 by Scott Hopkins, Lucius Luscher, and C. G. Upton, and in the convention of '85 by C. D. Dean, P. L. Soper, and C. E. Parker. In '83 and '84 it was represented by Maj. W. C. Ransom of Lambda, who, at the time of the founding of Alpha Nu, in 1872, was a resident of Lawrence and the chief promoter of the new chapter. The recent corresponding secretaries have been L. H. Leach, J. E. Curry, and W. T. Caywood. Two of the recent chiefs of the district, Scott Hopkins and C. F. Scott, are alumni of this chapter.

#### Admitted since August, 1881.

##### XLIII.

WARREN PERRY, Troy, Kas.

HENRY FREMONT SMITH, B. S. '85. Class leader; obtained faculty appointment for commencement day; assistant surveyor of Cowley county. Wellington, Kas.

WILSON SHERIDAN KINNEAR. Editor *Meade Centre Globe;* mayor of Meade Centre. Meade Centre, Kas.

CHARLES EDWIN PARKER. In '82–'83 was in Columbia School of Mines and member of Alpha Alpha; in '83 entered pharmacy department University of Michigan; member and cor. sec. of Lambda; graduated from department in '85; foreman of Leis Chemical Mfg. Co. Lawrence, Kas.

OLIVER DAVID WALKER, B. S. '83. On ball nine; graduated '86 at Keokuk Medical College with honors of class. Blue Mound, Kas.

##### XLIV.

GEORGE WILLIAM ROBINSON. Engineering, with headquarters at Denver, Col.

RALPH EMERSON STOUT. Reporter for Kansas City *Star.* Kansas City, Mo.

THOMAS W. HOUSTON. Real estate agent. Garnett, Kas.

##### XLV.

CHARLES ERNEST HALL. Real estate agent. Hutchinson, Kas.

OSCAR HENRY POCHLER, '88. Lawrence, Kas.

JOHN ATTIE SARGENT. Ticket agent Fort Scott & Gulf R. R. at Kansas City, Mo.

JOSEPH ELLSWORTH CURRY, '86. On football team; orator Orophilian Society in Oread-Orophilian contest; editor on *University Courier* and *University Review;* orator from senior class on Washington's birthday; cor. sec. Nortonville, Kas.

DEWITT CLINTON BOWER. Assistant cashier in bank. Delphos, Kas.

CLARENCE ERNEST WOOD, A. B. '84. Wamego, Kas.

##### XLVI.

HENRY LAWRENCE CALL, LL. B. '82. Topeka, Kas.

CHARLES FREDERICK FOLEY, LL. B. '84. Class leader; principal Armourdale schools. Armourdale, Kas.

ROBERT CRAWFORD RANKIN. Lawrence, Kas.

ARCHIBALD WATSON. Champion-prize winner on field day. Shawnee, Kas.

CHARLES DICKEY DEAN, B. S. '84. Class day orator; business manager and president of *Courier;* now city editor on *Lawrence Daily Journal.* Lawrence, Kas.

OLIN TEMPLIN, '86. Cockins prize in mathematics; debater Normal Society; assistant professor of mathematics; leader of class. Canon City, Col.

WEBSTER WILLIAM DAVIS. Orator in contest in Orophilian Society; land attorney and agent. Garden City, Kas.

CARL SMITH. With Day Theater Co., Canada. Home, Kansas City, Mo.

WILLIAM TALBOTT CAYWOOD, '89. Cor. sec. Vining, Kas.

EDWID FISKE STIMPSON, '88. Lawrence, Kas.

MARCUS N. BREMAN. McPherson, Kas.

##### XLVII.

FRANK EVERETT REED, '88. Orator on Orophilian contest. Newton, Kas.

THOMAS FRANCIS DORAN, '88. First prize in faculty declamatory contest; second *Courier* prize for chapel rhetoricals. Council Grove, Kas.

HARRY BUCKINGHAM, '89. Lawrence, Kas.

WALTER MOORE TOMLIN, '89. Winsfield, Kas.

LAWRENCE THEODORE SMITH, '89. Concordia, Kas.

JOSHUA BARLOW LIPPINCOTT, '87. Editor on *Courier;* on foot-ball team. Lawrence, Kas.

SAMUEL BURKHOLDER, JR., '86. Essay prize. Canada, Kas.

WILLIAM E. BORAH, '89. Lyons, Kas.

WILLIAM TELL REED, '87. Orophilian debater in Oread-Orophilian contest. Newton, Kas.

CAMPBELL McGEE WATSON, '90. Shawnee, Kas.

JOHN WEIGHTMAN, '87. Topeka, Kan.

## KENYON CHAPTER.

### [The Beta Alpha, at Kenyon College, Gambier, O.]

Kenyon College has nine professors and about sixty students. There are two courses, the classical and the philosophical, each composed wholly of prescribed studies. A theological seminary is connected with the college. A stone building for the library has been erected recently. Kenyon is the most important western institution belonging to the Protestant Episcopal church.

The fraternities are Delta Kappa Epsilon, Theta Delta Chi, Alpha Delta Phi, Psi Upsilon, Beta Theta Phi, and Delta Tau Delta. A chapter's membership varies from one to fifteen, the present average being about six.

The Beta Alpha, founded in 1879, has been successful, though meeting long-established rivals in a field by no means large enough for so many chapters. Its membership has averaged nine. The corresponding secretaries for the last four years and a half have been J. E. Good, E. M. Benedict, and G. C. Cox. The representatives at recent conventions have been C. D. Williams and W. K. L. Warwick in 1881; J. E. Good, W. S. Taylor, and A. M. Snyder in 1882; Good and Warwick in 1883; and R. B. Bloodgood, A. M. Snyder, and H. C. Ferris in 1884.

### Admitted since August, 1881.

#### XLIII.

WARREN EDWARD RUSSELL, '85. On ball nine and prominent in athletics; entered Amherst in '84 and became member of Beta Iota. Massillon, O.

MARTIN ARMSTRONG MAYO, '85. Editor-in-chief of *Advance*; now at Cincinnati Law School. Lima, O.

ALONZO MITCHELL SNYDER, A. B. '85. Inter-collegiate prize for best general athlete; editor *Reveille*; studying law. Galion, O.

ROBERT BENNETT WYNKOOP, '85. Division superintendent W. U. Telegraph. Crestline, O.

#### XLIV.

ERNEST MILNOR BENEDICT, A. B. '85. Editor of *Advance*; Phi Beta Kappa; honor man; cor. sec.; now surveying with C. & N. R. R. in Kentucky. Permanent address, 369 W. Seventh street. Cincinnati, O.; temporary address, Glasgow, Ky.

#### XLV.

EDWARD VANCE BOPE, A. B. '85. Now at law school of University of Michigan and member of Lambda. Findlay, O.

GEORGE CLARKE COX, '86. Kenyon Day orator; editor of *Reveille*; class president; cor. sec. Delhi, O.

HENRY CARR FERRIS, '87. Left Kenyon in '84, entered Stevens, and is member of Sigma. 337 Franklin street, Cleveland, O.

KENYON BRONSON CONGER, '87. Bicycle prize; editor of *Reveille*. Akron, O.

HARRY NEWTON HILL, '87. Engaged in iron and steel business. 3 Franklin Court, Cleveland, O.

GEORGE STRAIN COX, '87. Now at Chicago Medical College. Permanent address, Terre Haute, Ind.; temporary address, Twenty-sixth street and Paine avenue. Chicago, Ill.

CLEVELAND KEITH BENEDICT, '87. 369 W. Seventh street, Cincinnati, O.

CHARLES EVERITT TULLER. '87. Stock dealer at Dublin. Address, Dublin, O.

#### XLVI.

IRVING BOOTH TODD, '84. Editor of *Advance*; Phi Beta Kappa; valedictorian. Permanent address, Manhattan, Kas.; now at Frankfort, Ky.

ALBERT COUDON WHITAKER, '88. Now with Whitaker Iron Co. 2227 Chaplin street, Wheeling, W. Va.

FRANK HERSCHEL BRIGGS, '88. Painesville, O.

EBER THERAN TULLER, '88. Teaching. Dublin, O.

HARRY CURTIS DEVIN, '88. Mt. Vernon, O.

[The Beta Theta, at Madison University, Hamilton, N. Y.]

Madison University is a Baptist institution. It comprises a theological seminary, a college, and a preparatory school. In the college there are ten instructors and about one hundred students. Almost all of the students take the classical course of prescribed studies. The fraternities are confined to the college department. Delta Kappa Epsilon, Delta Upsilon, and Beta Theta Pi have chapters. Delta Kappa Epsilon owns a hall, and Delta Upsilon owns a chapter house.

The Beta Theta was founded in 1880 upon the basis of a local organization called the Adelphian Society. The names of such of the Adelphian alumni as have become members of the Beta Theta Pi since August, 1881, are inserted in the list of new members given below. The corresponding secretaries since the Chicago convention have been Walter Cook, C. J. Pope, C. C. Van Kirk, A. M. Dyer, and W. H. Crawshaw. E. D. W. Petteys was chief of the district in 1882-'83. C. J. Pope was at the convention of 1881; Dyer and C. E. Haworth at that of '82; Dyer, A. H. Cole, Van Kirk, and H. C. Lyman at that of '83; E. C. Harding, H. E. Slaught, and C. H. Douglass at that of '84.

## Admitted since August, 1881.

### XLIII.

CHARLES HENRY DOUGLASS, A. B., '85. Second Dodge entrance prize; second Lasher essay prize; editor-in-chief of *Madisonensis*; assistant professor in rhetoric, 1884-'85; valedictorian; Phi Beta Kappa; teacher. Delhi, N. Y.

REV. WILLIAM JOSIAH QUINCY, A. B., '76. Fourth Montgomery prize in oratory; Baptist minister. Broadalbin, N. Y.

REV. JUDSON KINCAID FOLWELL, A. B., '78. First Osborn mathematical prize; second Royce price in declamation; Phi Beta Kappa; Baptist minister. Bayonne, N. Y.

ALBION MORRIS DYER, A. B., '84. Cor. sec.; journalist. With *Evening Telegram*. Youngstown, O.

### XLIV.

DR. ELMER GARDINER KERN, Ph. B., '78. Studied at Hahnemann Medical College, Philadelphia; degree of M. D.; physician. Herkimer, N. Y.

REV. DAVID HART COOPER, '75. Studied in Carson College; Baptist minister. Waverley, N. Y.

REV. CHARLES PITMAN PEACHY FOX, A. B., '75. Royce prize declamation; Baptist minister. Washington, Kan.

REV. HARRY SCOTT SCHWARTZ, A. B., '76. Studied at University at Lewisburg; Baptist minister. Gouverneur, N. Y.

REV. MARTIN LA BURN RUGG, '80. Baptist minister. Salem, Oregon.

ALFRED BURT TAYLOR, '86. Merchant. Palmyra, N. Y.

ROBERT DOUGLASS BRIGGS, '86. Editor of *College Annual*, '86; farmer. Grand Ledge, Mich.

WILLIAM EDWARD WEED, '86. Second

Osborn mathematical prize; first Lasher essay prize; second Kingsford prize in declamation; editor of *Madisonensis*, 1885-'86. Clifton Park, N. Y.

### XLV.

FRANK AMNER GALLUP, '88. Third Dodge entrance prize. Sparta. Tenn.

WILLIAM HENRY CRAWSHAW, '87. First Allen essay prize; editor of *College Annual*, '86; editor of *Madisonensis*, 1885-'87; assistant professor of rhetoric; cor. sec., 1883-'86. 2521 North Front street, Philadelphia, Pa.

HOMER CHILD LYMAN, '87. Business manager of *Madisonensis*, 1885-'87. North Adams, Mass.

MARTIN REMINGTON NELSON, '86. Accountant's office of Michigan Central Railroad. Detroit, Mich.

### XLVI.

REV. ELDON HERBERT LOVETT, '75. Baptist minister. Long Island City, N. Y.

WILLIAM JAMES MOORE, '86. Studied at Columbia College. 125 Pennington street, Newark, N. J.

CHARLES CLARK PIERCE, '88. Walton, N. Y.

### XLVII.

ALBERT JOHN KIMMEL, '86. Studied at Denison University. Kendallville, O.

HENRY H. HAMILTON, '84. Lawyer. Rockford, Ill.

GEORGE HENRY MEYER, '89. Second Dodge entrance prize. Hamilton, N. Y.

HORACE GRANT McKEAN, '89. Angora, Philadelphia, Pa.

WILLIAM ANDRUS ST. JOHN, '87. Highland, Mich.

ALVAH EDWARD KNAPP, '89. Marblehead, Mass.

EDWARD MARSHALL VAN KIRK, '89. Greenwich, N. Y.

## MAINE STATE COLLEGE CHAPTER.

[The Beta Eta, at Maine State College, Orono, Me.]

The Maine State College of Agriculture and Mechanic Arts owes its origin to the national land grant, and is controlled by the state. By the will of the late ex-governor Abner Coburn it receives one hundred thousand dollars in 1886. There are courses in civil engineering and mechanical engineering, leading to the degree of B. C. E. and B. M. E.; and there are courses in agriculture, in chemistry, and in general science and literature, each leading to B. S. Almost all of the students choose the courses in civil engineering, mechanical engineering, and chemistry. Women are admitted, but only a few are in attendance. There are ten professors and about one hundred students.

The fraternities are Q. T. V., Beta Theta Pi, and Kappa Sigma.

The Beta Eta usually has about eighteen members. It was founded in 1878, upon the basis of the E. C., a society that dated from 1875. For several years it has published the college annual, *The Pendulum.* The recent corresponding secretaries have been C. S. Bickford, W. R. Pattangall, R. K. Jones, Jr., and J. D. Lazell. Jones is chief of the district. E. S. Abbot was at the convention of 1882; C. S. Bickford at that of 1883; and L. W. Taylor at that of 1884.

### Admitted since August, 1881.

#### XLIII.

WILLIAM PHILBROOK, '85, also '88. Bethel, Me.

#### XLIV.

CHARLES SAMPSON WILLIAMS, '85. Portland, Me.

FRANK EUGENE HULL, '85. Captain ball nine; editor *Pendulum;* class marshal; teacher. Warren, Me.

CLARENCE SUMNER LUNT, '84. Editor *Pendulum;* city editor *Whig and Courier.* Bangor, Me.

WILLIAM ROBINSON PATTANGALL, '84. Editor *Pendulum.* Campello, Mass.

FRANK ISSACHAR KIMBALL, '82. Valedictorian; division superintendent Penn. R. R. Greensburg, Pa.

WILLIAM MOREY, JR., '85. Editor *Pendulum;* U. S. Signal Office. Washington, D. C.

RALPH KNEELAND JONES, JR., '86. Editor *Pendulum;* editor-in-chief *Cadet;* captain Coburn cadets; cor. sec.; chief; class prophet. Bangor, Me.

FRED. WILLIAM DICKERSON, '85. Belfast, Me.

ELISHA CHICK VOSE, '85. Lawyer. Bangor, Me.

LEONARD GREGORY PAINE, '85. Editor *Pendulum;* class odist. Now at Stevens and member of Sigma. Bangor, Me.

#### XLV.

IRVING BURTON RAY, '86. Editor *Pendulum;* captain ball nine. Harrington, Me.

GEORGE FULLER BLACK, '86. Editor *Pendulum;* Editor *Cadet;* captain Coburn cadets; manager base-ball association; class historian. Palermo, Me.

HENRY TORSEY FERNALD, '85. On ball nine; editor *Pendulum.* Now at Wesleyan University. Middletown, Conn. Orono, Me.

EDWIN DWIGHT GRAVES, '86. Class odist. Orono, Me.

JAMES FREDERIC LOCKWOOD, '86. Coburn prize declamation, honorable mention; Prentiss prize essay, first prize, editor *Pendulum;* editor *Cadet;* class orator. Brewer, Me.

LUIS VERNET PRINCE CILLEY, '87. Buenos Ayres, Argentine Republic, S. A.

EDWIN VORANUS COFFIN, '87. Harrington, Me.

JAMES DRAPER LAZELL, '87. Cor. sec. Rockland, Me.

EUGENE CLARENCE BARTLETT, '86. Farmer. Orono, Me.

CHARLES LEON LIBBY, '86. Mechanical engineer. Bridgeport, Conn.

HARRY FOSTER LINCOLN, '88. Dennysville, Me.

#### XLVI.

CHARLES THATCHER VOSE, '87. On ball nine; editor *Cadet.* Middletown, N. B.

JAMES EDWARD DIKE, '76. One of the founders of the C. E. Grand Forks, Dak. Ter.

SIDNEY SMITH TWOMBLY, '86. Enfield, Me.

JAMES KENT CHAMBERLIN, '88. Sanitary engineer. Bangor, Me.

DAVID WILDER COLBY, '87. Editor *Cadet;* class historian. Skowhegan, Me.

CLAUDE LORRAINE HOWES, '88. Leader college orchestra. 700 Harrison avenue, Boston, Mass.

FRED. THAYER DREW, '88. Orono, Me.

#### XLVII.

JOHN RUSSELL BOARDMAN, '88. Editor *Cadet.* Augusta, Me.

FREDERIC LINCOLN THOMPSON, '89. Medical student. Augusta, Me.

ALPHONSO JOAN COFFIN, '89. Harrington, Me.

#### XLVIII.

WILLIAM HENRY SARGENT, '89. Brewer, Me.

CHARLES GRANVILLE CUSHMAN, '89. North Bridgeton, Me.

RALPH HEMENWAY MARSH, '88. Bradley, Me.

# UNIVERSITY OF MICHIGAN CHAPTER.

[The Lambda, at the University of Michigan, Ann Arbor, Mich.]

In the undergraduate department of the University of Michigan there are about six hundred students. The courses are largely elective. Degrees are conferred in arts, philosophy, science, letters, and engineering, the A. B. degree being the most popular. In the law, medical, pharmacy, dental, and graduate departments there are about a thousand students. Women are admitted upon the same terms as men. The university was established in 1841 and is controlled by the state.

In the order of original establishment the fraternities are Beta Theta Pi, Chi Psi, Alpha Delta Phi, Delta Kappa Epsilon, Sigma Phi, Zeta Psi, Psi Upsilon, Phi Kappa Psi, Delta Tau Delta, Phi Gamma Delta. Delta Upsilon is represented, and Sigma Chi is represented in the law department alone. Each of the departments, outside of the literary department, has one or more chapters of secret societies. Membership varies from ten to thirty. Most of the chapters occupy chapter houses. The Lambda was founded in 1845. It occupies a chapter house, No. 21 N. State street, where visiting Betas are always welcome. The recent corresponding secretaries have been J. A. Case, T. C. Phillips, C. E. Baker and W. T. Smith. In 1883-'84 Case was chief of the district. D. E. Osborn, D. A. Garwood, and W. B. Cady were representatives at the convention of 1881; J. A. Case, J. E. Beal, and J. H. Grant at that of 1882; J. E. Beal and D. K. Cochrane at that of 1883; Beal and E. L. Johnson at that of 1884, and at that of 1885 C. L. Andrews, F. L. Velde, and W. T. Smith, the last being the secretary of the convention. Major W. C. Ransom was at all of these conventions, except that of 1882, and was president of the convention of 1883.

### Admitted since August, 1881.

### XLIII.

CHARLES HENRY JAMES DOUGLASS. Initiated at Kappa; with Lambda three years; professor of history and English literature at Milwaukee high school. 168 Division street, Milwaukee, Wis.

EDWARD ADAMS BENSON. Came from Chi; spent a year in the law department. Milwaukee, Wis.

ALFRED CLAIBORNE DOWNS. Came from Epsilon; spent a year in the law department. Danville, Ky.

DAVID KIPLEN COCHRANE, '85. Did not graduate; editor *Chronicle*; now in business. Manistee, Mich.

FRED REYNOLDS BABCOCK, '85. Did not graduate; now in business. Manistee, Mich.

JAMES WILBER GREGORY, '86. Editor on '85's *Oracle*. Rockford, Ill.

### XLIV.

DWIGHT HORACE RAMSDELL, '86. Left college. Emery, Mich.

JESSE CORNELL SHATTUCK, '86. In business. Owosso, Mich.

FRANK JACOBS CHEEK, LL. B., '83. Came from Epsilon. Danville, Ky.

JOE WALKER COOPER. Came from Psi; spent a year in medical department. Wellsburg, W. Va.

ELBERT LELAND JOHNSON, Ph. B., '84. Came from Alpha Beta. Clay Center, Kan.

*WILLIAM WALTER HARRIS, '86. Lake Linden, Mich. Died January 16, 1884.

GEORGE WALTON WHYTE, '87. Editor *Oracle* of class of '86; editor *Chronicle*. Geneva Lake, Wis.

### XLV.

GEORGE LANPHERE PRICE, '86. Winner of a number of athletic prizes. Galesburg, Ill.

CHARLES EDWARD PARKER, Ph. C., '85. Cor. sec.; came from Alpha Nu. Home address, Ottawa, Franklin county, Kan.; temporary address, Lawrence, Kan.

DENVER JOHN MACKEY, '87. Was admitted at Theta under special dispensation; member of Theta Delta; studying law at Sandusky, Ohio.

WALTER TEIS SMITH, '87. Secretary of convention of '85; cor. sec.; came from Alpha Epsilon. Pekin, Ill.

FRANKLIN LUPPEN VELDE, '87. Came from Alpha Epsilon. Pekin, Ill.

CHARLES H. FORBES. Came from Omega; spent the year '83-4 in the law department of the University of Michigan; now at Harvard continuing law studies. Temporary address, 14 Mellen street, Cambridge, Mass.; home address, Durham, Cal.

CHARLES E. POWELL, A. M., '84. Came from Vanderbilt University and is a member of Beta Lambda; spent '83-4 in post graduate work; passed the civil service examination and was appointed to a clerkship in pension department. 131 street, N. E., Washington, D. C.

WILL COOPER HARRIS, '87. In business. Pontiac, Mich.

FRED. DAVID SHERMAN, '87. Grand Rapids, Mich.

JOHN HAZELTON COTTERAL, '87. In real estate business. Garden City, Kan.

### XLVI.

HOWARD GEORGE HETZLER, '86. Editor on *Palladium* of '86. Waterloo, Ia.

JAMES GABRIEL SMITH. Came from Alpha

Nu; studying law at the University of Michigan, 1611 Oak street, Kansas City, Mo.

CHARLES LINCOLN ANDREWS, '86. Chicago, Ill.

CLARENCE LEE DONYNS, '88. In business, Portsmouth, Ohio.

LOUIS BRIGGS LEE, '88. Brighton, Mich.

JED HANNIBAL LEE, '88. Brighton, Mich.

WILLIAM E. WOOD, '88. Accepted an appointment to West Point in '85; granted leave of absence on account of ill-health, and is now at Van Orin, Ill.

## XLVII.

JOHN HADLEY PATTERSON, '87. Class orator in freshman year; left college to become clerk of probate court. Pontiac, Mich.

EDWARD VANCE BOPE. In law department; came from Beta Alpha, Findlay, Ohio.

GEORGE CULLEY MANLY. In law depart-ment; came from Denver University and was a member of the Rho under special dispensation; was the Colorado representative at the inter-collegiate oratorial contest held at Columbus, O., in '85. Denver, Colo.

GEORGE B. WATSON. In law department; came from Alpha Nu. Shawnee, Kan.

ELLSWORTH E. OTIS. In law department; came from Alpha Gamma. Dundee, Ohio.

STERLING PARKS, '88. Came from Beta. Collamer, Ohio.

LOUIS ROSCOE DOUD, '89. Winona. Minn.

ROBERT SIMEON BABCOCK, '89. Manistee, Mich.

JULIAN MILLARD, '89. St. Paul, Minn.

DANIEL PHILIP GRANT, '89. Burlington, Ind.

FRED BERNARD SPAULDING, '89. Coldwater, Mich.

VICTOR MAXWELL TUTHILL, '89. Dowagiac, Mich.

# UNIVERSITY OF MISSISSIPPI CHAPTER.

### [The Beta Beta, at the University of Mississippi, Oxford, Miss.]

In the college department of the University of Mississippi the course for a degree covers five years, and there are about two hundred and fifty students. There is also a law department. The university is a state institution. Women are admitted.

There are chapters of the Rainbow, Delta Kappa Epsilon, Delta Psi, Sigma Chi, Phi Kappa Psi, Chi Psi, Sigma Alpha Epsilon, Phi Delta Theta, and Beta Theta Pi.

The Beta Beta was established in 1879 upon the basis of Alpha Kappi Phi. W. H. Clark, J. M. Steen, J. Y. Murry, Jr., G. T. Fitzhugh, J. D. Burge, and H. M. Quin have been the corresponding secretaries since 1881. J. C. Harris, Dabney Marshall, and W. L. Birdsong were at the convention of 1882; and Dabney Marshall was the poet of the convention of 1885.

### Admitted since August, 1881.

#### XLIII.

JOHN YOUNG MURRY, JR., '83 and law '84. Editor-in-chief *University Magazine* '83; on the editorial staff of *Daily Clarion* during session of legislature '86; practicing law. Ripley, Miss.

HERBERT RUFFIN COCKE, '85. Brandon, Miss.

WILSON GAINES RICHARDSON, '85. Sherman, Tex.

HILLRIE MARSHALL QUIN, '86. First freshman medal at commencement of '84; anniversarian for Hermæan Literary Society February 22d, '86; exchange editor of *University Magazine* '86. McComb City, Miss.

JAMES SWAPTURE GADBERRY, '85. Lawyer. Brookhaven, Miss.

FRANK MAY SCOTT, '82 law. Came from Omicron; first honor man of law class; lawyer. Rosedale, Miss.

WILLIAM TIDENCE LANE CLARK. '84. McKinney, Tex.

GUSTON THOMAS FITZHUGH, '86. Bohemian medalist '83; first honor man freshman year; second honor man sophomore year; first sophomore medalist; junior first honor man, and junior speaker; editor of *University Magazine* '86; valedictorian of the graduating class. Oxford, Miss.

WILL TATE McDONALD, '82 law. Third honor man of law class; member of Mississippi legislature. '86; lawyer. Ashland, Miss.

JAMES BONEDIAN ROSS, '86. In business. Jackson, Miss.

THOMAS ARTHUR CHICHESTER, '86. Bookkeeper. Edwards, Miss.

#### XLIV.

REV. WILLIAM ISIDORE SINNOTT, '78. Member Alpha Kappa Phi. Oxford, Miss.

DR. JOHN JACKSON RHODES, '77. Member of Alpha Kappa Phi; physician. Brandon, Miss.

EDWARD EVERETT FRANTZ, '78. Member of Alpha Kappa Phi; editor and proprietor of *Brandon Republican.* Brandon, Miss.

ADOLPHUS EVANS BROWN, '87. Brandon, Miss.

ROBERT LOVE McLAURIN, '86. Attended South-western Presbyterian University. Brandon. Miss.

JOHN HARVEY JOHNSON, '86. Attended medical college Louisville, Ky. Brooklyn, Mass.

OLIVER NEWTON KILLOUGH, '87. In business. Vandale, Ark.

LOUIS THOMAS FITZHUGH, JR., '88. First Philomathean medalist '84. Oxford, Miss.

WILLIAM RANDOLPH HILL, '87. First-medal man of freshman and sophomore classes at commencements of '84 and '85. Jackson, Miss.

#### XLV.

RICHARD PETTUS MOORE, '86 law; second honor man of freshman class of '83; first of sophomore of '84; then left college and returned in the law class of '86; editor of *University Magazine.* Columbia, Miss.

AMZI WADDLE HOOKER, '85. Lexington, Miss.

LOUIS KARR SHARPE, '88. Natchez, Miss.

THOMAS SPENCE SHARPE, '87. Natchez, Miss.

JOHN DAVID BURGE, '86; second freshman medalist '84; editor-in-chief *University Magazine* '86. Oxford, Miss.

EDWARD LEE LASHBROOKE, '87. New Orleans, La.

JOSEPH WILLIAMS CHALMERS, '88. In business at Memphis, Tenn.

MALCOLM CAMERON MONTGOMERY, '87. Natchez, Miss.

NICHOLAS STUBBS WALKER, '87. In business at Brownwood, Tex.

HARRIS CHRISTIAN HOOVER, '88. McComb City, Miss.

SIMON SUGGS MATHEWS, '86. Oxford, Miss.

ALBERT LEWIS PITTMAN, '88. Studying law. Columbus, Miss.

#### XLVI.

WILLIAM WEBSTER MAYES, '88. Hazlehurst, Miss.

ALONZO MONROE HARLEY, '87. Atlanta, Miss.

JAMES BASSETT McELROY, '87. Teaching at Mayhew Station, Miss.; permanent address, Columbus, Miss.

ROBERT FINLEY COCHRAN, '85 law. First honor man and valedictorian; editor of the *University Magazine.* Meridian, Miss.

ANDREW BROWN LEARNED, '87. Now at Vanderbilt and a member of Beta Lambda. Natchez, Miss.

SAMUEL HOLLOWAY, '89. Oxford, Miss.

ROBERT BURNS MAYES, '88. In business at Hazlehurst, Miss.

### XLVII.

WALTER HARRIS, '89. Ripley, Miss.

EDWARD LEANDER BARKER McCLELLAND, '89. West Point, Miss.

JOHN BASCOM COCHRAN, '86. Meridian, Miss.

THADDEUS BOOTH LAMPTON, '89. Columbia, Miss.

## NORTHWESTERN CHAPTER.

[The Rho, at Northwestern University, Evanston, Ill.]

Northwestern University is managed by the Methodist Episcopal church. In the college department it has twelve instructors and, including women, about one hundred and fifty students. There is a preparatory department. Schools of theology, medicine, and law are intimately connected with the university, although, to some extent, they are under separate management. The medical and law departments are in Chicago. The others are in Evanston, a suburb.

There are chapters of Phi Kappa Psi, Sigma Chi, Phi Kappa Sigma, Beta Theta Pi, and Delta Upsilon. Membership varies from ten to twenty-five.

The Rho was founded in 1873. A. G. Briggs, F. E. Lord, D. H. Bloom, W. D. Fullerton, C. S. Tomlinson, and C. N. Zeublin have been the recent corresponding secretaries. W. A. Hamilton and D. H. Bloom have been chiefs of the district. F. H. Thatcher, J. T. Hatfield, and W. A. Hamilton were delegates to convention in '81; J. C. Bannister in '82; and W. D. Fullerton in '84.

### Admitted since August, 1881.

#### XLIII.

EDWARD B. LANIER, '86. Came from Theta. Bloomington, Ill.

JOHN POLLARD McWILLIAMS, '85. In business. Dwight, Ill.

CLINTON SAMUEL TOMLINSON, '86. On ball nine; editor-in-chief of college annual; cor. sec.; on Evanston *Index*: now editing *Boone County Republican*. Boone, Ia.

SAMUEL LAMBERT BODDY, '85. Business manager of college annual; studying law. Cherokee, Ia.

#### XLIV.

WILLIAM DYER FULLERTON. A. B. '85. Cor. sec.; teaching. Present address, 560 McMillan street, Cincinnati, O.; permanent address, Ottawa, Ill.

SAMUEL ROBERT SLAYMAKER, '86. Now at Chi. Beloit, Wis.

HENRY HAMILL, '87. Editor-in-chief of *Syllabus* (college annual). Blunt, Dak.

ELBERT REYNOLDS TILLINGHAST. '86. Mann declamation, second prize; pitcher on ball nine; now at Yale, '88. Temporary address, 44 Elm street, New Haven, Conn.: permanent address, Hope Valley, R. I.

WILLIAM EDWARD DAVIDSON, '86. Now at Chicago Congregational Theological Seminary. Lafayette, Ill.

EDWARD DUNN HUXFORD, '85. On ball nine; president base-ball association '85; first honor at graduation. Cherokee, Ia.

CASSIUS MARCELLUS WEEDMAN, '87. Came from Theta. Farmer City, Ill.

#### XLV.

LOUIS RICH, '86. Now reporter on Englewood *Call*. Englewood, Ill.

FRANK EDWIN MILLER, '88. In business in Chicago. Address, Evanston, Ill.

JOHN ADAMS, '87. Yorkville, Ill.

HENRY RAND HATFIELD, '87. Evanston, Ill.

BOND STOWE, '87. President of base-ball association, and on the nine. Evanston, Ill.

#### XLVI.

CHARLES GEORGE LEWIS, '87. On base-ball nine. Evanston, Ill.

HARVEY BROWN, '87. Gage debate prize. Evanston, Ill.

JOSEPH B. HUBBARD, '85 law. Practicing law. Evanston, Ill.

HARVEY REEVES CALKINS, '88. Evanston, Ill.

GEORGE BUCKLEY DEEM, '87. Spring Hill, Kas.

JOHN EDDY HUNT, '88. Ashton, Ill.

#### XLVII.

EARL MONTGOMERY CRANSTON. Under dispensation; A. B. University of Denver, '85; studying law. 190 W. Fourth street, Cincinnati, O.

ARTHUR ROBIN EDWARDS, '88. 2816 Indiana avenue, Chicago, Ill.

WILLIAM AUGUSTUS MOORE. Under dispensation; A. B., University of Denver, '85. Denver, Col.

WILLIAM SEWARD ILIFF. Under dispensation; member of '87 at University of Denver. Santa Cruz, Cal.

CLARENCE JOSEPH WHITE. Under dispensation; class of '88 at University of Denver. Georgetown, Col.

GEORGE CULLY MANLY. Under dispensation; A. B., University of Denver, '85; now at Lambda. Chillicothe, O.

ALFRED TRUMAN MOORE. Under dispensation; class of '88 at University of Denver. Denver, Col.

WILLIAM JOY CADY. Under dispensation; '88 in Denver. Care L. F. Waldo, Shelby, Mich.

EDMUND CHASE QUEREAU, '88. Reporter on Evanston *Index*. Aurora, Ill.

JAMES CLARK TISDALE, '89. Rock Springs, Wy. T.

HERBERT FISK BRIGGS, '89. Napa City, Cal.

CHARLES NEWTON ZEUBLIN, '87. Cor. sec.; on base-ball nine; manager base-ball association; came from University of Pennsylvania. 243 Michigan avenue, Chicago, Ill.

PHILIP RAYMOND SHUMWAY, '89. Evanston, Ill.

FRANK COLE WHITEHEAD, 89. Evanston, Ill.

JOHN B. YOUNG, '89. Elgin, Ill.

## OHIO STATE UNIVERSITY CHAPTER.

### [The Theta Delta, at Ohio State University, Columbus, Ohio.]

The Ohio State University belongs to the state and is managed by a board of trustees appointed by the governor. The origin of the institution was the national land grant for the support of agricultural and mechanical colleges. The proceeds of Ohio's share of the grant amounted to more than five hundred thousand dollars. The income of this fund is enjoyed by this university; and there is also an annual appropriation made by the legislature. The grounds and buildings, now worth some five or six hundred thousand dollars, were in part the gift of the city and county. Degrees are conferred in arts, philosophy, science, mechanical engineering, mining engineering, civil engineering, and agriculture. There are about one hundred and fifty undergraduates, and about the same number in the preparatory department. Women are admitted. Since the institution was opened, in 1873, it has been steadily growing in favor.

Phi Gamma Delta, Phi Kappa Psi, Sigma Chi, Chi Phi, Phi Delta Theta, and Beta Theta Pi have chapters, the membership varying from ten to fifteen.

The Theta Delta was founded upon the basis of a local society, the Phi Alpha. The petition was sent to the chapters in the short way permitted by the constitution, and on the 11th day of December, 1885, the chapter was established. The corresponding secretary is W. C. Sabine. W. G. Hyde of Theta Delta is college secretary of the fraternity.

### XLVII.—The Founders.

WILLIAM REED POMERENE, '85. Debater in '85 vs. '86 contest, and also in Alcyone-Horton contest; *Makio* editor; admitted at Alpha Lambda; now at Cincinnati Law School. Coshocton, O.

DENVER JOHN MACKEY, '85. Admitted at Theta by dispensation in 1883, and member of Lambda; law student. Sandusky, O.

CHARLES HERBERT HIRST, '86. Admitted at Theta by dispensation in 1883. Clerk with Peter Horn & Co. 29 Fifth street, Pittsburg, Pa.

EDWARD CYRUS BENEDICT, '85. Admitted at Theta by dispensation in 1883; paper dealer. Dayton, O.

CHARLES VERNON PLEUKHARP, '85. Admitted at Theta by dispensation in 1883; orator in '85 vs. '86 contest, and also on Washington's birthday celebration in '83; business manager of *Lantern*; vice-president inter-state oratorical association; traveling salesman for Jas. Pleukharp & Co. 80 W. Third avenue, Columbus, O.

ELMER ELLSWORTH PAINE, '85. Admitted at Theta by dispensation in 1883. City editor *Daily Torch-Light*, Xenia, O.

CLAYTON WILLIAM DELAMATRE, '84. Admitted at Beta Kappa; first honor orator in local contest and second honor in state contest; now at Cincinnati Law School. Kimball, O.

WILBY GRIMES HYDE, '87. Admitted at Beta Kappa; essayist Alcyone anniversary; fraternity and personal editor *Lantern*; at convention of '85, representing Phi Alpha petition; marshal of same; secretary of Ohio Beta Theta Pi Association, and college secretary of the fraternity. New Holland, O.

WILBUR HENRY SIEBERT, '87. Washington's birthday orator in '85. 235 S. Front street, Columbus, O.

WALLACE CLEMENT SABINE, '86. Class prophet; cor. sec. 1520 N. High street, Columbus, O.

HERBERT TAYLOR STEPHENS, '88. Editor-in-chief of *Lantern*; second honor orator in local contest for '85; ranking captain battalion of cadets. Adrian, Mich.

HENRY JULIAN WOODWORTH, '87. *Makio* editor; Washington's birthday orator, '84; Alcyone anniversary orator. Jefferson, O.

FRANK MILTON RAYMUND, '89. Akron, O.

GAIUS GLENN ATKINS, '88. Admitted at Alpha Gamma. Columbus, O.

CHARLES EDWARD SKINNER, '90. Admitted at Beta Kappa. Redfield, O.

JULIUS FLOTO, '89. 101 Molitor street, Cincinnati, O.

### OHIO UNIVERSITY CHAPTER.

[The Beta Kappa, at Ohio University, Athens, O.]

The Ohio University was founded in 1804, and is the oldest college northwest of the Ohio river. There are eight instructors. In the college department there are about forty students. There is also a preparatory department. Women are admitted. The institution is managed by a board of trustees appointed by the governor of the state. The university has four buildings. The library contains over 8,000 volumes. The chemical and physical laboratories are well equipped.

Beta Theta Pi, Delta Tau Delta, and Phi Delta Theta have chapters. The size of a chapter varies from five to twelve. Preparatory students are admitted by all of the fraternities.

The Beta Kappa was established in 1841 and has a long roll of distinguished men. W. F. Boyd was the representative at the convention of 1881; R. U. Wilson at that of 1882; C. W. De Lamatre at that of 1884; and W. G. Hyde at that of 1885. Hyde is now college secretary. C. S. Coler, H. H. Humphrey, C. W. De Lamatre, G. W. Reed, E. B. Skinner, and Chas. H. H. Higgins have been the corresponding secretaries since 1881. W. F. Boyd of the Beta Kappa has for several years been a member of the board of directors.

**Admitted since August, 1881.**

#### XLIV.

WILLIAM FRANK GORDON, '86. Book-keeper. Portsmouth, O.

PHELPS LEETE, '86. Book-keeper. Portsmouth, O.

JOHN ELLSWORTH DILLON, '86. Teacher. Permanent address, McArthur, O.

WILBY GRIMES HYDE, '86. College secretary; now at Ohio State University, and member of Theta Delta. New Holland, O.

#### XLV.

CALVIN HUMPHREY, '88. Contest essayist of Athenian Society '86. Coolville, O.

GEORGE WASHINGTON REED, '88. Contest debater of Philomathean Society at commencements of '85 and '86; cor. sec. Uhrichsville, O.

LAWRENCE GRANT WORSTELL, '89. Tappan, O.

#### XLVI.

ERNEST BROWN SKINNER, '88. Cor. sec. Redfield, O.

LEWIS McCLELLAN GILLILAN, '88. Cor. sec. Jackson, O.

CHARLES HENRY HIGGINS, '87. Contest essayist of Philomathean Society '85; editor of *Philomathenian;* cor. sec. Athens, O.

CHARLES EDWARD SKINNER, '89. Now at Ohio State University, and member of Theta Delta. Redfield, O.

HERBERT RUSSEL McVAY, '89. Editor of *Philomathenian.* Athens, O.

#### XLVII.

ADELBERT GRANT JOHNSON, '89. Portage, O.

CHARLES HOOD FONTS, '90. Meigs Creek, O.

JOHN MARCELLUS JOHNSON, '89. Trimble, O.

# OHIO WESLEYAN CHAPTER.

## [The Theta, at Ohio Wesleyan University, Delaware, O.

In the college department of the Ohio Wesleyan University there are about two hundred men and one hundred and thirty women. There is a preparatory department. According to the laws of the university, the fraternities are not allowed to initiate or to pledge students of the preparatory department. There are chapters of Beta Theta Pi, Phi Delta Theta, Phi Kappa Psi, Delta Tau Delta, Phi Gamma Delta, and Chi Phi. A chapter of Sigma Chi existed from 1855 to 1884 and was then suppressed by the faculty.

The Theta has had a continuous existence ever since its founding in 1853. G. P. Thorpe, N. H. Fairbanks, F. P. Irvin, and S. P. Withrow have been the recent corresponding secretaries. Thorpe was chief of the district in 1884-'85. In the last few years, S. G. Williams, W. O. Robb, and E. Wambaugh have been editors of the BETA THETA PI, and Williams, Robb, and Dr. T. A. Reamy have been members of the board of directors. There have been the following representatives at recent conventions: J. Alexander and C. M. C. Weedman, 1881; J. R. Hughes, N. H. Fairbanks, and M. S. Milligan, 1882; W. O. Robb and N. H. Fairbanks, 1883; T. R. Terwilliger and M. G. Park, 1884; M. G. Park, 1885. In 1883 five students of the Ohio State University were initiated under a special dispensation. Their names are given in the roll of the Theta Delta.

### Admitted since August, 1881.

#### XLIII.

ETHELBERT CLARENCE RANDOLPH, '85. Lincoln, Ill.

JOHN PETERS McCABE, '83. Permanent address, Delaware, O.; temporary address, Germantown, O.

CHARLES ALFRED DOE, Columbus, O.

BERTHOLD ALEXANDER WILLIAMS, '84. Winton Place, Hamilton county, O.

#### XLIV.

THOMSON RITCHIE TERWILLIGER, '84. At the Ohio Medical College, Cincinnati, O. Permanent address, Mt. Pisgah, Clermont county, O.

MELVIN LEE MILLIGAN, '84. Editor of *Bijou* '84; reading law in Columbus, O. Permanent address, Deavertown, O.

FRANK PERRY IRVIN, '86. Editor-in-chief of *Transcript;* class orator on Washington's birthday in '84; on ball nine; cor. sec.; now a member of Delta. Piqua, O.

MILFORD GRANT PARK. '86. On lecture committee; on ball nine; major of battalion, '84. Permanent address, Galion, O.; temporary address, Seffner, Fla.

JAMES TIVIS PICKERING, '83. Teacher. Permanent address, Pickerington, O.; temporary address, New Holland, O.

CHARLES CLAYTON PICKERING, '83. Studying law. Permanent address, Pickerington, O.; temporary address, Cincinnati, O.

WILLIAM ALFRED BALDWIN, '85. Delaware, O.

ARTHUR MERCIAN MANN, '85. Local editor of *Transcript;* on the oratorical contest; came from Alpha Gamma; studying law. Middleport, O.

JOHN WILLIS ADAIR, '84. Initiated at Alpha Gamma; studying medicine. London, O.

#### XLV.

WILLIAM BELKNAP McARTHUR, '86. Out of college. Memphis, Mo.

EDWARD LINCOLN SHANNON, '89. Teaching. Permanent address, Xenia, O.; temporary address, W. Middleburg, O.

GEORGE ROBERT PEEBLES, '85. Fayette, Ia.

SQUIRE ROBINSON GREER, '86. Business manager of *Transcript;* cor. editor; now a member of Delta. Oxford, O.

DURWARD STARR GRIFFIN, '86. Business manager of *Transcript;* orator on Zetagathean Society Annual; cor. editor. Delaware, O.

#### XLVI.

SAMUEL POTTENGER WITHROW, '87. Local editor-elect of *Transcript;* cor. sec.; Ohio Wesleyan vice-president of the state association for the year '86. Jacksonborough, O.

JOHN HARDIN WATERHOUSE, '88. Delaware, O.

ERNEST ASHTON SMITH, '88. Piqua, O.

GEORGE ADDISON TALBERT, '88. Beaver Dam, Wis.

FRANCIS MERRICK STARR, '85. Druggist. Delaware, O.

#### XLVII.

FRANKLIN THEODORE PENNINGTON, '86. Valedictorian on Zetagathean Society Annual; business manager of *Transcript;* junior orator Washington's birthday, '85; now a member of Delta. Tiffin, O.

FRANK LEMAR YOUNG, '89. Mt. Vernon, O.

DANIEL HENRY SOWERS, '89. Westville, O.

FREDERICK THEODORE JONES, '89. Employed in the Deposit Bank. Delaware, O.

EUGENE QUENTIN STARR, '89. Delaware, O.

CHARLES SKINNER MANLY, '88. Denver, Colo.

HARRY LESLIE LAMONT WEBB, '89. Steubenville, O.

## UNIVERSITY OF PENNSYLVANIA CHAPTER.

### [The Phi, at the University of Pennsylvania, Philadelphia, Pa.]

The University of Pennsylvania was established in 1755. Its college or undergraduate department comprises courses in arts, science, philosophy, finance and economy, and music. The university also has departments of law, medicine, dentistry, veterinary medicine, and biology. In the course in arts there are one hundred and thirteen students; in science, two hundred and eight students; in philosophy, twenty; in finance, twenty-seven; in music, twelve; making a total of three hundred and eighty students for the college department. The total number of students in all departments is one thousand and twenty-eight.

The fraternities are Zeta Psi, Phi Kappa Sigma, Delta Phi, Delta Psi, Phi Kappa Psi, Beta Theta Pi, Alpha Tau Omega, and Chi Phi. Chi Phi has no representation in the college department. Phi Gamma Delta is believed to be dead.

The Phi was founded in 1880, and usually has about thirteen members. Since 1881 the corresponding secretaries have been H. S. Stetler, F. H. Edsall, and R. S. Maison. Stetler has been chief of the district. C. R. Claghorn was at convention in 1881; and Stetler, W. E. Maison, and R. S. Maison in 1883.

### Admitted since August, 1881.

#### XLIII.

CHARLES RICK DUNDORE, '85. Banking. Present address, New York City; former address, 1424 Girard avenue, Philadelphia, Pa.

HENRY LIPPINCOTT PATTERSON, '85. Studying law. 640 N. Fifteenth street, Philadelphia, Pa.

WILLIAM EMOTT MAISON, '85. Took honors every year; editor on *Record* of '85; orator on commencement; now at General Theological School in New York City. Temporary address, corner Twentieth street and Ninth avenue, New York, N. Y.; permanent address, 6901 Woodland avenue, West Philadelphia, Pa.

DR. THOMAS BUDD BRADFORD, '84, med. A. B., Princeton, '81. Present address, Episcopal Hospital, Philadelphia, Pa.; home, Dover, Del.

#### XLIV.

HOWARD ATLEE DAVIS, '83 law. 1206 Spring Garden street, Philadelphia, Pa.

*SAMUEL EDWARD SCOTT, '82. Graduated with honors; commencement orator. Home was Philadelphia, Pa. Died in 1883.

DR. NATHAN PENROSE GRIMM, '85 med. Appointed resident physician at Children's Hospital, Philadelphia, in '85; appointed physician at Episcopal hospital in March, '86. Residence, 217 W. Miner street, West Chester, Pa.

#### XLV.

DR. HOBART AMORY HARE, '84 med. Thesis prize; Fiske fund prize of the R. I. State Medical Society in June, '85; now matriculate in veterinary department; assistant in physical diagnosis; attending physician in the dispensary for diseases of children. 113 S. Twenty-second street, Philadelphia, Pa.

DR. JOHN MARION BRADFORD, '84 med. Eighth and Cumberland streets, Philadelphia, Pa.

WILLIAM ROBINSON COCHRANE, '85 med. Ph. B., Western University of Pennsylvania,'82; on state geological survey. 75 Fourth avenue, Pittsburg, Pa.

FRANK HYNARD EDSALL, '85 med. Now studying in Europe. Hamburgh, Sussex county, N. Y.

ROBERT STEPHEN MAISON, '87. 6901 Woodland avenue, West Philadelphia, Pa.

DR. CALVIN JONES IRVIN, '85 med. 1900 N. Thirteenth street, Philadelphia, Pa.

#### XLVI.

DR. GUSTAV ADOLPH RENZ, '84 med. Degrees of Ph. G. and M. D. Corner Summit avenue and Oxford street, St. Paul, Minn.

DR. MARK HALFPENNY LINCOLN, '85 med. Laurelton, Pa.

DR. FRANKLIN MORE STEPHENS, '85 med. Honorable mention and M. D. '85. Home, Bentleysville, Pa.; present address, Oswego, N. Y.

HENRY PRICE BALL, '87. Honors in '86. 4533 Frankford avenue, Philadelphia, Pa.

FREDERICK COLTON CLARKE, '87. 134 N. Twenty-first street, Philadelphia, Pa.

ALFRED WEEKS, JR., '86. 4051 Locust street, Philadelphia, Pa.

JOHN PHILIP KRECKER, '87. 134 N. Twenty-first street, Philadelphia, Pa.

#### XLVII.

DR. LOUIS P. COATES, '85 med. Carlett P. O., Va.

GEORGE FETTEROLF, '87. Address, Girard College, Philadelphia, Pa.

#### XLVIII.

GEORGE CLAY BOWKER, '88. Was manager-in-chief of *University Magazine*. 4375 Main street, Manayunk, Philadelphia, Pa.

GEORGE ALBERT FREYER, '86 law. 518 Walnut street, Philadelphia, Pa.

## RANDOLPH MACON CHAPTER.

### [The Xi, at Randolph Macon College, Ashland, Va.]

Randolph Macon College, founded in 1832, is the property of the Methodist Episcopal church, South. The students are not divided into classes. Degrees are conferred in arts, philosophy, and science. There are eight instructors and about one hundred and twenty-five students. Women are not admitted.

Southern Kappa Alpha, Phi Kappa Sigma, Beta Theta Pi, Sigma Chi, and Kappa Sigma Kappa have chapters.

The Xi, was founded in 1873. Its recent corresponding secretaries have been R. E. L. Holmas, H. L. Stuart, G. T. Patton, and Geo. Shipley. M. H. Albin was at convention in 1882, and H. L. Stuart in 1884.

### Admitted since August, 1881.

#### XLIII.

HARRY LEE STUART, '85. Orator at the annual debate and medalist of Franklin Literary Society, '81–'82; declamation prize Franklin Literary Society, '83–'84; English prize, '83–'84; editor *Randolph Macon Monthly:* cor. sec.; practicing law. Gainesville, Tex.

ROBERT WINFREE, '87. Lynchburg, Va.

#### XLIV.

OTHO FRED. MEARS, '86. Public debater of the Washington Literary Society, '82; now at University of Virginia. Pungoteague, Va.

HENRY LEE WINFREE, '86. In business. Lynchburg, Va.

GEORGE TAZEWELL PATTON, '86. Cor. sec.; now in business in Richmond. Permanent address, Ashland, Va.

JAMES LINDSAY PATTON, '86. Ashland, Va.

#### XLV.

PERCY ROWE, '86. Orator; public debater Washington Literary Society, '84; manager *Randolph Macon Monthly;* teaching. Permanent address, Bowling Green, Va.; temporary address, Murfreesboro, N. C.

MUSCOL LIVINGSTONE SHACKELFORD, '86. Editor *Monthly:* public debater and orator, '86. 1413 I street, Washington, D. C.

THOMAS JACKSON BLAND, '88. Studying medicine. Little Plymouth, Va.

JOHN SUMMERFIELD HOBSON, '88. In business. Lynchburg, Va.

#### XLVI.

GARLAND BUFFINGTON, '88. Out of college. Huntington, W. Va.

PETER CLINE BUFFINGTON, '89. Huntington, W. Va.

ROBERT WILLIAMS PATTON, '89. Ashland, Va.

PEYTON BROWNE WINFREE, '89. Lynchburg, Va.

#### XLVII.

GEORGE SHIPLEY, '87. Cor. sec.; manager *Randolph Macon Monthly.* Moorefield, W. Va.

CHARLES CARROLL HERING, '88. Public debater, '86. Cross Keys, Va.

JORDAN JOSIAH LEAKE, '89. Ashland, Va.

WILLIAM ANDREW GIBBONS, '89. Yancey, Va.

## RICHMOND CHAPTER.

### [The Alpha Kappa, at Richmond College, Richmond, Va.]

In the undergraduate department of Richmond College there are eight professors and about one hundred and fifty students. The only degrees are those of A. B. and A. M. The students are not divided into classes. The college is chiefly a Baptist institution.

The fraternities are Beta Theta Pi, southern Kappa Alpha, Phi Kappa Sigma, Phi Delta Theta, Kappa Sigma Kappa, Phi Alpha Chi, and Sigma Alpha Epsilon.

The Alpha Kappa dates from 1870. Tracy McKenzie, W. R. Thomas, E. B. Pollard, and G. B. Stacy have been the corresponding secretaries since the Chicago convention. J. G. Field, Jr., and E. B. Pollard have been chiefs of the district. M. B. Curry attended convention in '81; W. R. Thomas in '82; and C. D. Roy and P. Y. Tupper in '85.

#### Admitted since August, 1881.

#### XLIII.

JAMES ARTHUR BORUM, '83. Portsmouth, Va.

FRANK DEWEY TABB, '83. Portsmouth, Va.

W. WARREN TALLEY, A. B. '84. Editor *Messenger;* afterwards with Omicron; now at Medical College of Virginia, Richmond, Va.; home, Lynchburg, Va.

WILLIAM RUSSELL THOMAS, '83. Cor. sec. 113 E. Grace street, Richmond, Va.

AMZI WADDLE HOOKER. Afterwards with Beta Beta. Lexington, Miss.

#### XLIV.

GEORGE WASHINGTON QUICK, A. B. '85. Editor *Messenger;* debater's medal; essay medal; final orator '85. Temporary address, Theological Seminary, Chester, Penn; home. Farmwell, Va.

ALEXANDER MCIVER BOSTICK, A. B. '85. Editor *Messenger;* Gain medalist; essay medal. Lawtonville, S. C.

LAFAYETTE RUPERT HAMBERLIN, '84. Editor *Messenger;* Steel medalist; Woods medalist; valedictorian; teaching. Shreveport, La.

#### XLV.

EDWARD BAGBY POLLARD, '86. Editor *Messenger;* Steel medalist; improvement in debate medal; essay medal; valedictorian; cor. sec. and chief of district. 2316 E. Grace street, Richmond, Va.

HENRY HERBERT HARRIS, JR. Address, Richmond College, Richmond, Va.

THOMAS NEAL FERRELL, '85. Base-ball nine. Danville, Va.

ALFRED BAGBY, JR., A. B. '85. Tanner medalist. Teaching at Mechum's River, Va.; home. Stevensville, Va.

WILLIAM ROBERT FITZGERARLD, '85. Danville, Va.

LEROY SPRINGS LYON, '86. 13 S. Fifth street, Richmond, Va.

WILLIAM ELAM TANNER, JR., '89. 216 S. Third street, Richmond, Va.

#### XLVI.

FRANK LYON, '85. 13 S. Fifth street, Richmond, Va.

CHARLES DUNBAR ROY, '87. Editor *Messenger.* 18 Ellis street, Atlanta, Ga.

ROBERT ALEXANDER CUTLER, '88. 802 W. Marshall street, Richmond, Va.

#### XLVII.

GEORGE BEN STACY, '88. Initiated at Psi. 406 E. Cary street, Richmond, Va.

ALEXANDER MITCHELL CARROLL. '88. Asheville, N. C.

CURTIS LEE LAWS, '89. Aldie, Va.

CORNELIUS TIMOTHY SMITH, JR., '89. Childsburg, Va.

RUSSELL CHAMPION WILLIAMS, '88. 709 W. Grace street, Richmond, Va.

## RUTGERS CHAPTER.

### (The Beta Gamma, at Rutgers College, New Brunswick, N. J.

Rutgers College, founded as Queen's College in 1770, was formerly controlled by the Reformed (Dutch) church in America, but is now unsectarian. It has in the college proper seventeen professors and one hundred and twenty students. There is under the management of the college a preparatory school, which has about the same number of students as the college. A theological seminary is also closely connected with the college.

The fraternities are Delta Phi, Zeta Psi, Delta Upsilon, Delta Kappa Epsilon, Chi Phi, Beta Theta Pi, and Chi Psi. Class societies are Alpha Phi (junior), Kappa Alpha Sigma (sophomore), and Gamma Phi (freshman).

The Beta Gamma was founded in 1871 as the Alpha of Alpha Sigma Chi. R. J. Wortendyke, J. W. McKelvey, L. F. Ruf, and E. M. Alden have been the corresponding secretaries since 1881. Dr. W. H. Watson was a director for the three years ending in 1883.

### Admitted since August, 1881.

#### XLIII.

WILLIAM HENRY BARNES, '85. Business manager of the *Targum*; Cook mineralogical prize; Phi Beta Kappa; address to the president class day. East Hampton, N. Y.

#### XLIV.

CHARLES WILLIAM HARRISON, '85. Was special student in chemistry, and not a candidate for a degree; on ball nine; now studying medicine. Verona, N. J.

JOHN BARTLETT ALDEN, '82. Spader prize for essay on modern history, and several minor prizes; editor of *Targum*; now on the editorial staff *Brooklyn Times*. Brooklyn, N. Y.; former address, Hoosick Falls, N. Y.

LAWRENCE EDMUND McCABE, '87. Took sophomore prize for oratory in Philo; was one of the editors of the *Scarlet Letter*; member of junior society. East Hampton, N. Y.

ARTHUR COYLE PAYNE, '85. Phi Beta Kappa; prize for best thesis at graduation; planter of ivy, class day. College Point, L. I., N. Y.

#### XLV.

FRANK WILLIAM RIBBLE, '86. East Millstone, N. J.

#### XLVI.

SAMUEL DE WITT DRURY, '89. Rhinebeck, N. Y.

HENRY LIVINGSTONE RUPERT, '88. Member of freshman and sophomore societies. East Millstone, N. J.

EDWIN MOORE ALDEN, '88. Took freshman prize for oratory in Peitho; cor. sec.; member and associate founder of freshman society; member of sophomore society. Hoosick Falls, N. Y.

WALTER ALMER BARROWS, JR., '88. Special student in chemistry; member and associate founder of freshman society; member of sophomore society. Mt. Holly, N. J.

ISAAC WRIGHT REYNOLDS, '88. Member of freshman and sophomore societies. Montrose, N. Y.

#### XLVII.

SAMUEL DODDS, '88. Special student in chemistry; member of freshman and sophomore societies. Anna, Ill.

ALBERT BODWELL HARRISON, '89. Irvington, N. J.

JOSEPH BORDEN REYNOLDS, '86. Phi Beta Kappa; has an appointment for class day. Bordentown, N. J.

## ST. LAWRENCE CHAPTER.

### [The Beta Zeta, at St. Lawrence University, Canton, N. Y.]

St. Lawrence University is the only Universalist college in New York. It embraces a college and a theological school. In the college there are six instructors and about sixty students. Women are admitted.

Beta Theta Pi and Alpha Tau Omega are the fraternities. They have halls in the college buildings.

The Beta Zeta was founded in 1875. For several years it published the college annual, *The Gridiron*. It has many peculiar traditions, and is one of the most enthusiastic chapters in the fraternity. The recent corresponding secretaries have been Geo. S. Conkey, Frank T. Post, Arthur E. Forbes, A. B. Church, and E. S. K. Merrell. Forbes has been chief of the district. The chapter was represented at the convention of 1881 by W. Fitzgibbons; at that of 1882 by Conkey and Post; at that of 1883 by C. M. Baker, R. E. Sykes, and Geo. B. Helmle; at that of 1884 by Helmle; and at that of 1885 by R. P. Barnes.

### Admitted since August, 1881.

#### XLIII.

GEORGE BERNARD HELMLE, B. S. '85. Russell prize for oratory, and Parker prize for composition; military editor and reviser of *Brooklyn Times*. Brooklyn, E. D., N. Y.

CLEMENT MORELLE BAKER, B. A. '85. Instructor of Latin in the college. Canton, N. Y.; former address, Whitney's Point, N. Y.

#### XLIV.

ARTHUR ELBRIDGE FORBES, B. S., '85. Cor. sec. and chief; editor of the *Oxford Democrat*. Paris, Me.

RODNEY PERCY BARNES, '86. Madrid, N.Y.

AUGUSTUS BYINGTON CHURCH, '86. Rich prize in oratory. Sherborne, N. Y.

HOLTON DANIEL ROBINSON, '86. Massena, N. Y.

*FREDERIC FRANCIS AMIE LIOTARD, '86. Canton, N. Y. Died 1883.

#### XLV.

NOBLE HENRY ADSIT, B. S. '84. Student of medicine. Potsdam, N. Y.

HENRY MARSHALL SMITH, '87. Has left college. Boston, Mass.

WILLIAM THOMAS CRISLER, '87. Petersburg, Ky.

JOHN A. CRANSTON, '87. Madrid, N. Y.

THOMAS E. DALTON, '87. Russell prize in oratory. Chase's Mills, N. Y.

WARNER BONNEY MATTESON, '87. First Rich prize in oratory. Hermon, N. Y.

JOHN W. RAFFERTY, '87. Second Rich prize in oratory. West Pierrepont, N. Y.

#### XLVI.

WILLISTON MANLEY, '88. Second Russell prize in oratory. Canton, N. Y.

EDGAR SANFORD KEEN MERRELL, '87. Present cor. sec.; third Rich prize in oratory. Lonville, N. Y.

FRANK YALE ADAMS, '88. York mathematical prize of '85. Whitney's Point, N. Y.

WILLIAM GAINES, '87. Burlington, Ky.

#### XLVII.

JOHN MONTGOMERY RICH, '87. Canton, N. Y.

CHARLES AVERILL RICH, '87. Canton, N.Y.

EVERETT CALDWELL, '89. Canton, N. Y.

HENRY ALLEN ABBOTT, '89. West Sumner, Me.

JOHN MURRAY ATWOOD, '89. Canton, N. Y.

## STEVENS CHAPTER.

### [The Sigma, at Stevens Institute of Technology, Hoboken, N. J.]

Stevens Institute is a school of mechanical engineering, well known in engineering circles throughout Europe and America. Mathematics, physics, and chemistry, with a vast amount of practical work in the physical, electrical, mechanical, and chemical laboratories and the work-shop, are its specialties: but there is also full instruction in modern languages, English, mechanical drawing, etc. The course is of four years and leads to the degree of mechanical engineer. There are fourteen instructors and about one hundred and seventy-five students. There is also a preparatory department.

There are chapters of Theta Xi, Delta Tau Delta, Beta Theta Pi, Sigma Chi, Chi Psi, and Chi Phi.

The Sigma was founded in 1875. H. F. Mitchell. R. L. Fearn, C. A. Hall. Rollin Morris, E. G. Coldewey, and J. L. Coker. Jr., have held the position of corresponding secretary since 1881. Pierce Butler and W. R. Baird attended the convention in '81, the latter being secretary: Butler and T. G. Smith, Jr., in '82; Fearn, E. F. Lewis, O. H. Baldwin, W. S. Dilworth, and Baird in '83; G. E. Cook and E. G. Coldewey in '84; and Hall and Smith in '85. Baird has been a chief of district, an editor of the magazine, and historiographer. Fearn is now an editor of the magazine.

### Admitted since August, 1881.

#### XLIII.

MOSES YALE BEACH. '85. Editor *Eccentric:* now editor *Daily Graphic.* New York, N. Y.

EDWARD FOX LEWIS. '85. On foot-ball team: *Eccentric* editor; is now draughting for Farrel Foundry and Machine Co. Waterbury, Conn.

THOMAS GARDINER SMITH, JR.. M. E., '85. On lacrosse team; *Bolt* editor: cor. sec.: now with the St. Louis & Pittsburgh division of the Pa. R. R., at Indianapolis, Ind. Home. Oak street, Cincinnati. O.

#### XLIV.

OSCAR HOWARD BALDWIN. M. E., '85. Foot-ball captain; with Phineas Jones & Co. Newark, N. J.

EDWARD FRANCIS WHITE, '86. Came from Beta Gamma. Bergen Point, N. J.

GEORGE EDWARD COOK, '86. In business, Canton, O.

CORNELIUS JAMES FIELD, '86. Business manager of lacrosse team, glee club, *Bolt,* and *Indicator.* Brooklyn, N. Y.

JOHN CHATELLIER, '86. In business. New York, N. Y.

ROLLIN NORRIS, M. E., '85. Cor. sec.: lacrosse captain; with Bartlett. Hayward & Co., Baltimore, Md. Home, Ilchester, Md.

GEORGE FLEMING SANDT, M. E., '84. A. B., Lafayette College, '82; with Edison Electric Light Co., New York, N. Y. Home, Easton, Pa.

WILLIAM OLIVER BARNES, M. E., '84. *Bolt* editor; with Barnes & Peel, Paterson, N. Y.

LEWIS BAKER, JR., '86. Now editor of St. Paul *Reporter,* St. Paul, Minn; former address, Wheeling, W. Va.

#### XLV.

FRANK ALLEN MAGEE, M. E., '83. With the Commercial Tel. Co., New York, N. Y.

HENRY BANNER EVERHART, '86. *Bolt* editor. Montgomery, Ala.

HENRY LAWRENCE GANTT, M. E., '84. Lacrosse team; from Alpha Chi; with Poole & Hunt, Baltimore. Md.

WILLIAM COMBE POST, '86. Foot-ball team; lacrosse captain. Jersey City Heights, N. J.

CHARLES ANDREWS HALL, '87. Cor. sec.; lacrosse team. Mobile, Ala.

#### XLVI.

DRUID ALEXANDER WALTON. '87. Louisville, Ky.

HENRY ABBEY. M. E., '85. Lacrosse team; *Bolt* and *Indicator* editor; Soltmann prize for draughting; with Cowles Electric Smelting Co., Lockport, N. Y. Home. Cleveland, O.

EDWARD GEORGE COLDEWEY. '87. Cor. sec.; foot-ball and lacrosse teams; now at Sheffield Scientific School. '87. Present address. New Haven. Conn.; home. Louisville, Ky.

HARRY CARR FERRIS, '88. Foot-ball and lacrosse teams; came from Beta Alpha. Cleveland, O.

WILLIAM CLARK HAWKINS, '88. Lacrosse team. Taunton, Mass.

RANDOLPH MOORE ISAAC, '88. Lacrosse team; record of 100 yard dash, one-quarter mile run, and standing broad jump; left college. Towson, Md.

JAMES LIDE COKER, '88. Cor. sec.: *Indicator* editor. Darlington, S. C.

#### XLVII.

MILLARD CALDWELL HAMILTON, '88. Omaha, Neb.

RUSSELL HUMPHREY SMITH, '88. Initiated at Alpha Pi. Chicago, Ill.

LEONARD GREGORY PAINE, '86. Initiated at Beta Eta. Bangor, Me.

JAMES HENRY SHELDON. '89. Foot-ball team. Hoboken, N. J.

EDWIN MAY DRUMMOND, '88. Louisville, Ky.

ALEXANDER WOLFGANG MACK, '88. Raritan, N. J.

LEWIS CHARLES MACK, '89. Raritan, N. J.

## UNION CHAPTER.

### [The Nu, at Union College, Schenectady, N. Y.]

Union College was founded in 1795. In 1873 it absorbed a medical school, a law school, and an observatory, all situated in Albany; and since then the official name of the institution has been Union University. The college department has eighteen instructors and about one hundred and forty students. There are prescribed classical, scientific, and engineering courses. The institution is not controlled by any religious denomination; and the name is intended to signify that in establishing the college several denominations co-operated.

The fraternities are Kappa Alpha, Sigma Phi, Delta Phi, Psi Upsilon, Delta Upsilon, Alpha Delta Phi, Beta Theta Pi, and Phi Delta Theta. Chapters have from six to fifteen members.

The Nu was founded in 1881, and its corresponding secretaries have been J. W. Adams, F. D. Hall, W. H. Robinson, and K. C. Radliff. Hall has been chief of the district. Adams attended convention in 1882; J. R. Van Ness, Hall, and A. B. Bishop in 1883; and Hall in 1884.

### Admitted since August, 1881.

#### XLIII.

JAMES ROBERTSON VAN NESS, '83. Commencement orator; prize for best examination in U. S. constitution; editor of *Garnet;* practicing law. Permanent address, Osborne's Bridge, Fulton county, N. Y.; temporary address, Northville, N. Y.

ALVORD CALVIN EGELSTON,'83. Junior essay prize; commencement orator; editor of *Concordiensis;* teaching. Permanent address, Gloversvil'e, N. Y.; temporary address, Homewood, Cook county, Ill.

GEORGE WILLIAMSON VAN VRANKEN, '85. Left Union at end of sophomore year; entered class of '86 at Cornell and became a member of Beta Delta. Address, Lisha's Kill, N. Y.

#### XLIV.

WILLIAM HENRY ROBINSON, '85. Cor. sec.; left Union at the end of junior and entered the class of '85 at Princeton College; now at Princeton Theological School. West Hebron, N. Y.

ALVIN BARBER BISHOP, '85. Commencement orator; second Blatchford prize; class poet; editor of *Garnet;* Phi Beta Kappa; teaching. Warwick, N. Y.

FRANCIS ELIHU CRANE,'85. Commencement orator; Schenectady, N. Y.

CORNELIUS WELLS DE BAUN, '86. Left college and enter d class of '86 at Albany Medical College. Fonda, N. Y.

WILLIAM FRANKLIN SHICK,'86. Left Union and entered class of '86 at Lafayette. Easton, Pa.

#### XLV.

KELTON C. RADLIFF, '87. Cor. sec.; vice-president junior class. Schenectady, N. Y.

NELSON JOSEPH GULICK, '87. Broadalbin N. Y.

JOHN ERICSSON CLUTE, '87. Editor *Garnet;* left Union and entered class of '88 at Columbia Medical College, where he is now a member of Alpha Alpha. Schenectady, N. Y.

#### XLVI.

JULIUS THEODORE WILLIAM KASTENDIECK, '87. Left Union and is now studying medicine in the New York Homeopathic College. Schenectady, N. Y.

DOW VROMAN, '87. Editor of *Garnet.* Middleburgh, N. Y.

WILLIAM FRAZIER PETERS, '88. Left college at end of first term freshman year. Ripley, O.

FRANK HOPKINS SILVERNAIL, '88. Valatie, N. Y.

FRANK DUDLEY LEWIS, '88. Editor of *Concordiensis.* Amsterdam, N. Y.

ALLEN J. DILLINGHAM, '88. Schenectady, N. Y.

GEORGE WEED BARHYDT, '88. Clerk of U. C. Senate; second Allen essay prize; now studying for the ministry at Middletown, Conn. Schenectady, N. Y.

#### XLVII.

PHILIP HENRY COLE, '88. Red Hook, N. Y.

EDWARD BERNARD COBURN,'88. Troy, N.Y.

ARTHUR MOUL HARDER, '87. Troy, N. Y.

NORMAN DAVID FISH, '89. Ballston Spa, N. Y.

ROBERT HOOSICK WASHBURNE, '89. Ballston Spa, N. Y.

Vanderbilt University was founded in 1873. It is controlled by the Methodist Episcopal Church, South. Besides the college departments there are schools of theology, law, medicine, pharmacy, and dentistry. There are about three hundred students in the college department. There is no division into college classes. Degrees are conferred in arts, philosophy, science, and engineering. Women are not admitted. There are about four hundred students in the professional schools. In the whole university there are about fifty instructors. The grounds and buildings are very attractive. The endowment is nearly one million dollars.

The fraternities are Phi Delta Theta, Kappa Sigma, the Rainbow, southern Kappa Alpha, Beta Theta Pi, Sigma Alpha Epsilon, Chi Phi, and Sigma Nu. Membership varies from six to twenty-five. The authorities were for years hostile to fraternities; but all restrictions were removed in 1883.

The petition from Vanderbilt was before the fraternity for several years. On account of the anti-fraternity laws the petition could not be granted. From time to to time the Cumberland chapter was, by dispensation, allowed to elect and initiate Vanderbilt men. As soon as the hostile laws were repealed, the petition was sent to the chapter in the short way. It was granted, and on February 23d, 1884, the Beta Lambda was established. The corresponding secretaries have been C. L. Jungerman, J. B. Ellis, J. H. Harris, A. J. Barbee, and Alfred Hume. Jungerman and Ellis have been chiefs of the district. Jungerman, J. J. G. Ruhm, and W. T. Guild attended the convention of 1884.

### XLVI.—The Founders.

(XLIV.)

HENRY EUGENE HARLAN. Member of the Beta Beta. Macon. Miss.

ROBERT PETER WHITESELL, B. L., '83. Lawyer, firm Harpole & Whitesell. Union City, Tenn

CHARLES LEE JUNGERMAN. B. E., '83. Cor. sec ; chief. Architect. Cole building. Nashville, Tenn.

CHAS. E. K. S. POWELL. B. A., '83. Philosophic improvement medal. '82; studied law at University of Michigan, and graduated at Columbian Law School. Washington, D. C.

JOSEPHUS CONN GUILD, '83. Prize scholarship in engineering; architect and engineer. Chattanooga, Tenn.

LINN WHITE, B. E., '83, C. E., '84. Paducah, Ky.

WILLIAM EDWARD MYER. Scholarship ($100); merchant. Carthage, Tenn.

EDWARD HAMILTON BOWSER. Prize scholarship in engineering; gymnasium instructor, '82-'83; engineer. McMeekin, Fla.

GEORGE WASHINGTON BLACKWELL. Bartlett, Tenn.

EDWARD WAIDE THOMPSON. Prize scholarship in chemistry; studied chemistry at University of Pennsylvania; with the firm of Thompson & Kelly. Nashville, Tenn.

JOHN HARRIS KELLEY. Prize scholarship in chemistry; assistant instructor in chemistry at Vanderbilt University, '85-'86; chemist with Nashville Fertilizer Co. Nashville, Tenn.

CHARLES CHRISTMAS BURROWS. Merchant. Morrilton, Ark.

EUGENE JACKSON BUFFINGTON. Merchant. Covington, Ky.

ALBERT SIDNEY JOHNSTON DUDLEY. Contestant for Young medal, '83. Richmond, Va.

SAMUEL COLE WILLIAMS, B. L., '84. President of Dialectic: B A. '81 and valedictorian of Humboldt College; Moot Court representative, '84; lawyer, firm of Rawlins & Williams, Humboldt, Tenn.

JOHN JACOB GREGORY RUHM. Studied chemistry at University of Illinois; now at Cumberland studying law. Nashville, Tenn.

CHILTON A. McDONALD. Versailles, Ky.

JAMES WILLIAM McCLURE. Cor. sec.; medal in mathematics at Central University, Ky.; commercial traveler. Temporary address, Cincinnati, O.; permanent address, Winchester, Ky.

HARRY LEE BRANNON, M. D., '85. One year at Emory College; physician. Eufaula, Fla.

THOMAS PETTUS BRANCH, B. E., '86. Prize scholarship in engineering; engineer. Cuthbert, Va.

(XLV.)

JOE BLACKBURN ELLIS, B. A., '85. Fellow in English, '85-'86; cor. sec.; chief; chief marshal of V. U., '82-'83; business manager of Observer. Glasgow, Ky.

COLEMAN CLARKE SLAUGHTER, B. A., '85. President of Dialectic; vice-president of State Oratorical Association; contestant for Dialectic medal; teacher. Present address. Woolwine High School, Nashville, Tenn.; permanent address, Hopkinsville, Ky.

JOSEPH ALEXANDER ALTSHELER. Scholarship in Latin; reporter on Louisville Courier-Journal. Louisville, Ky.

ALLEN GARLAND HALL, B. L. '83. Contestant for Founder's medal in oratory; president of Greenville, Ala., Female College '83-'84; lawyer. Cole building, Nashville, Tenn.

CHAS. WESLEY BEALE, M. A., '81, B. L., '83. Founder's department medals in academic, '81, in law, '83; Owen prize medal, '81; prize scholarship in natural history and geology; fellowship in natural history and geology; lawyer. Cole building, Nashville, Tenn.

CHAS. LEWIS THORNBURG, B. S. '81, B. E. '82, C. E. '83, Ph. D. '84. Prize scholarship in scientific course; fellow in mathematics '81-'83; fellow in engineering '83-'84; assistant instructor in engineering since '84. Vanderbilt University, Nashville, Tenn.

WM. ALLEN PUSEY, B. A. '85. Class representative; scholarship in Greek; president of Dialectic; fellow in history, '85-'86. Elizabethtown, Ky.

LEE CRUCE. Contestant for Young medal and Dialectic anniversarian; lawyer. Marion, Ky.

ROBERT F. HIBBITT. High trapeze athlete '84. Louisville, Ky.

EDWARD BENJAMIN DAVIS. At Ohio Wesleyan '82-'83; artist and chemist. Nashville, Tenn.

CHAS. ADOLPHUS CALDWELL. Now at the Rensselaer Polytechnic Institute, Troy, N. Y., studying architecture. Macon, Ga.

BENJAMIN F. TAYLOR. Business manager of *Observer;* now on the New York *World.* New York, N. Y.

NEWTON WORTH BONHAM. Franklin, Mo.

WILLIAM THOMPSON GUILD. Contestant for Philosophic medal '85 and for Dialectic medal '86. Nashville, Tenn.

CHILES CLIFTON FERRELL, B. A. '85. Fellow in Greek '85-'86. Hopkinsville, Ky.

## XLVI.

ALFRED HUME, '87. Captain eng'neering base ball club; cor. sec. 518 Woodland street, Nashville, Tenn.

JOHN McPHERSON LAUDER. Graduated with first hon r at Wofford College; scholarship and fellowship in natural history and geology; teaching. Williamston, S. C.

JAMES ALEXANDER HARRIS, '86. Contestant for declaimer's medal '84; representative of class of '86; representative of Dialectic Literary Society in inter-state oratorical contest; cor. sec. Jonesboro, Tenn.

JOHN L. W. SLAUGHTER. Lawyer. Owenton, Ky.

JAMES PERRIN SMITH. Graduated at Wofford College; fellow in natural history and geology; pitcher on ball nine. Spartanburg, S. C.

JOHN BROOKS ROBERTSON, '88. Guilford, Ind.

ALLAN JONES BARBEE, '87. Cor. sec.; merchant. Ripley, Tenn.

JOSEPH ANDREW GUTHRIE, '88. Versailles, Ky.

WRIGHT HUNTER, '86. Louisville, Ga.

AUSTIN L. PREWETT, B. L. '85. Lawyer. Columbia, Tenn.

TYLER CALHOUN, '88. Nashville, Tenn.

## XLVII.

GRANVILLE ALLISON, '88. Nashvil'e, Tenn.

WILLIAM CHARLES BRANHAM, '86. Contestant for Dialectic declaimer's medal. Nashville, Tenn.

ANDREW BROWN LEARNED, '89. Member of the Beta Beta. Natchez, Miss.

JOHN LYLE SUMMERS, '86 law. A B. and valedictorian, Emory and Henry College, '84; clerk of Vanderbilt Moot Court. Morristown, Tenn.

WILLIAM BLYTHE WARD, '89. Jefferson, Tex.

WM. ROBERTS PATTEN, '89. Chattanooga, Tenn.

LUCIUS SALISBURY MERRIAM, '89. Chattanooga, Tenn.

ALFRED BROWN PUSEY, '89. Elizabethtown, Ky.

## XLVIII.

ROBERT DONALD GOODLETT, JR., '89. Nashville, Tenn.

WALTER GILL KIRKPATRICK, '86. Scholarship in mathematics; Owen prize medal; fellowship in engineering. Nashville, Tenn.

# UNIVERSITY OF VIRGINIA CHAPTER.

[The Omicron, at the University of Virginia, University of Virginia Post-office, Va.]

At the University of Virginia the courses of study are not prescribed and the students are not divided into classes. Each branch of instruction is termed a school. Thus there are the schools of Latin, Greek, modern languages, moral philosophy, mathematics, and so on. In each school there are several classes. Each student studies in such schools as he pleases; but if he expects to receive a degree he must finally complete in the several schools a course that is practically equivalent to the course that would secure the same degree in an ordinary college. This system originated in this university, and is found in many southern institutions. In the department of medicine there are about one hundred students; in the department of law, about eighty-five; and in the literary and scientific department about two hundred.

The fraternities are Beta Theta Pi, Delta Kappa Epsilon, Phi Kappa Sigma, Phi Kappa Psi, Sigma Alpha Epsilon, Phi Gamma Delta, Chi Phi, Sigma Chi, Delta Psi, Mystic Seven, Kappa Sigma, Pi Kappa Alpha, Alpha Tau Omega, southern Kappa Alpha, Phi Delta Theta, and Kappa Sigma Kappa.

The Omicron was founded in 1850. From the beginning, and especially in recent years, it has been largely composed of members coming from other colleges. C. B. Parkhill, N. R. Clarke, M. H. Albin, W. W. Talley, and W. F. McLeod have been the corresponding secretaries since 1881. W. N. Smith, W. C. White, and N. R. Clarke have recently been chiefs of districts. W. M. Atkinson was at convention in 1881; C. Skinner in 1882; J. E. Heath in 1883; W. C. White and H. C. Warren in 1884; and G. R. Lockwood in 1885. C. M. Hepburn, of Omicron, was, for several years, an editor of the BETA THETA PI.

## Admitted since August, 1881.

### XLIII.

DR. CORNELIUS SKINNER. Initiated at Epsilon. Louisville, Ky.; former address. Danville, Ky.

WILLIAM HOWARD PERKINSON. Initiated at Alpha Phi. Petersburg. Va.

JOHN RANDOLPH TUCKER, JR. Editor of *Virginia University Magazine;* initiated at Pi Rho. Richmond. Va.

RICHARD BROOKS MAURY, JR. Memphis, Tenn.

ALEXANDER TAYLOR PATTON. Initiated at Alpha Theta. Bentivoglio, Va.

*OBADIAH JENNINGS WISE. Initiated at Alpha Theta. Gordonsville, Va. Died in 1884.

### XLIV.

NORBORNE ROBERTSON CLARKE. Cor. sec. and chief; initiated at Alpha Mu. Demopolis, Ala.

MARTIN HIRST ALBIN. Bachelor of law '84; cor. sec.; initiated at Xi. St. Paul, Minn.; former address, Winchester, Va.

### XLV.

CHARLES FORD WOODS. Initiated at Alpha. Mu. Carthage, Ala.

JOHN JOSEPH ATKINSON. Initiated at Zeta. Gonzales. Tex.

BENJAMIN JAMES FITZPATRICK. Montgomery. Ala.

DAVID THORNTON EDWARDS. Bachelor of law, '85; initiated at Epsilon. Versailles. Ky.

JAMES WILLIAM KERN. Degree of Ph. D. '85. White Post. Va.

### XLVI.

THOMAS SHIELDS LYON. Bachelor of law '84. Galveston, Tex.

WILLIS HENRY BOCOCK. Initiated at Zeta. Hampden Sidney College, Va.

CHARLES EMORY JOHNSON. Initiated at Pi. Evansville, Ind.

DANIEL LYON HEATH. Initiated at Beta Beta. Coma, Miss.

ROBERT EDWARD LEE HOLMES. Bachelor of law '85; initiated at Xi. Ivor, Va.

ALEXANDER WATKINS TERRELL. Initiated at Xi. Lynchburg, Va.

WILLIAM WARREN TALLEY. Cor. sec.; initiated at Alpha Kappa. Lynchburg, Va.

ANDREW JACKSON MONTAGUE. Bachelor of law '85; initiated at Alpha Kappa. Jamaica, Va.

WILLIS FIELD McLEOD. Cor. sec. Versailles. Ky.

## WABASH CHAPTER.

[The Tau, at Wabash College, Crawfordsville, Ind.]

Wabash is a Presbyterian college that was founded in 1832. It confers degrees in arts and in science. The courses are partially elective. There are twelve instructors and about one hundred and twenty undergraduates. There are also about seventy preparatory students. Women are not admitted.

There are chapters of Beta Theta Pi, Phi Delta Theta, Phi Gamma Delta, Phi Kappa Psi, and Sigmi Chi.

The Tau dates from 1845. The corresponding secretaries since the Chicago convention have been J. F. Statesman, R. S. Thomson, and Parke Daniels. W. H. Kent and J. E. Williamson were the representatives at the convention of 1881; Statesman at that of 1882, and Chas. Wilson at that of 1884.

### Admitted since August, 1881.

#### XLIII.

MORTON HENRY INSLEY, '85. Second prize sophomore declamation; left college at the end of sophomore year. Crawfordsville, Ind.

#### XLIV.

HERBERT RITCHIE HESS, '83. Student of law. Indianapolis, Ind.

PARKE DANIELS, '87. Prep. declamation prize, first; freshman declamation prize, first; on inter-society exhibition; editor of *Wabash*; cor. sec. Rockville, Ind.

#### XLV.

FREDERICK JAMES BIPPUS, '88. Huntington, Ind.

FREDERICK WASHINGTON COOK, JR. Baldwin prize essayist; came from Pi; now studying at Heidelberg, Germany. Evansville, Ind.

DAVID HOWARD MAXWELL, '86. On society exhibition; sophomore declamation prize, first; junior essay prize, first; Baldwin prize essayist; came from Pi. Rockville, Ind.

SHERMAN ALLEN TROUT, '88. Prep.

declamation prize, second; left college at end of freshman year. Crawfordsville, Ind.

JOHN WILLIAM DOAK, '87. Sophomore declamation prize, second; on foot-ball eleven; now studying law; will resume college studies next year with '88. Paris, Ill.

#### XLVI.

HARRY GREENE, '88. Class officer. Crawfordsville, Ind.

ARTHUR ALBERT McCAIN, '89. Prep. declamation prize, second. Crawfordsville, Ind.

JESSE AUSTIN GREENE, '89. Class officer. Crawfordsville, Ind.

LOUIS PERKINS CAIN, '90. Danville, Ill.

#### XLVII.

HOWE ALLEN CONDIT, '90. Terre Haute, Ind.

JOHN WESLEY KIEFF, '87. On foot-ball eleven; on inter-society contest exhibition; editor of *The Wabash*. Lafayette, Ind.

STANLEY CARNAHAN HUGHES, '89. Class officer. Richmond, Ind.

FRANK HARRISON BOUDINOT, '90. Terre Haute, Ind.

## WASHINGTON AND JEFFERSON CHAPTER.

[The Gamma, at Washington and Jefferson College, Washington, Pa.]

Jefferson College at Cannonsburg and Washington College at Washington were, in 1865, united under the name of Washington and Jefferson, and Washington was made the site of the consolidated college. The institution is controlled by the Presbyterian church. The college department has eight instructors and about one hundred and fifty students. There is also a preparatory department. Women are not admitted.

There are chapters of Beta Theta Pi, Phi Gamma Delta, Phi Kappa Psi, Phi Kappa Sigma, Delta Tau Delta, Phi Delta Theta, and Alpha Tau Omega.

The Gamma was founded in 1842 at Jefferson College. A chapter was founded at Washington College in 1855. Upon the union of the colleges the chapters were consolidated. Since the convention of 1881 the corresponding secretaries have been J. S. Taylor, C. E. Irwin, J. M. Clarke, M. S. McKennan, and R. M. Brownson. R. P. Patterson and R. Harvey Young were delegates at the convention of 1881; and Patterson at that of 1884. R. Harvey Young was for years the general treasurer and a member of the board of directors.

**Admitted since August, 1881.**

### XLIII.

WILLIAM CAMPBELL JACOB, '83. Wellsburg, W. Va.

### XLIV.

JOHN McCRACKEN THOMPSON, '86. Washington, Pa.

WILLIAM McKENNAN, '86. Washington, Pa.

ROBERT HAZLETT CUMMINS, '86. Wheeling, W. Va.

### XLV.

ROBERT McKENNAN BROWNSON, '85. Cor. sec. Washington, Pa.

CLARENCE B. BAGULEY, '87. Wheeling, W. Va.

THOMAS RAMSEY McKENNAN, '89. Cor. sec. Washington, Pa.

### XLVI.

MOORE STOCKTON McKENNAN, '89. Cor. sec. Washington, Pa.

WILLIAM JAMES FREDERICKS, '85. Burgettstown, Pa.

OLIVER McCLELLAN CAMPBELL, '85. Belleville, Pa.

SAMUEL JACOB, '86. Wellsburg, W. Va.

### XLVII.

WALTER WORTHINGTON MEDILL, '86. Tiltonville, O.

JAMES DAVID JACK, '88. Carmon. Pa.

RUSH THOBURN JONES, '88. Washington, Pa.

WILLIAM ABSALOM BAIRD, '89. Washington, Pa.

BURT ALLISON BROWN, '89. Marchand, Pa.

## WESTERN RESERVE CHAPTER.

[The Beta, at Western Reserve University, Cleveland, O.]

The undergraduate department of Western Reserve is called the Adelbert College of Western Reserve University. For many years that department was at Hudson and was called Western Reserve College. The change of name and of location was made in 1882. In the college there are ten instructors and about one hundred students. Women are admitted. The university has a medical department at Cleveland and preparatory departments at Hudson and Green Springs. The Case School of Applied Science is in the immediate neighborhood of Adelbert College and answers the purpose of a scientific department; but, although it is managed in sympathy with the university, its government is wholly independent and it is not properly a department of Western Reserve.

Alpha Delta Phi, Beta Theta Pi, Delta Upsilon, Delta Kappa Epsilon, and Delta Tau Delta have chapters in Adelbert. The membership varies from five to fifteen.

The Beta was established in 1841, just three months before the Ohio University chapter. N. C. Stevens, J. A. Rohbach, G. M. Fletcher, and L. A. Sadler have been the recent corresponding secretaries. Rohbach was chief of the district. Stevens was at convention of 1881; W. B. Parmelee and J. W. Andrews in 1882; Andrews in 1883; and Fletcher in 1884.

#### Admitted since August, 1881.

##### XLIV.

THADDEUS DAY McFARLAND, '85. Hudson, O.

JAMES THOMAS LEES, '86. Phi Beta Kappa; Greek oration; editor *Reserve*. Elmwood, Ill.

SOLON LOUER, '86. Now at Alleghany College. Willoughby, O.

GEORGE MARCUS FLETCHER, '85. Studying law. Geneva, O.

CHARLES ALDEN WASHBURN, '86. Pittsfield, Mass.

##### XLV.

CHARLES JONES, '84. Mining engineer. Seattle, Wash. Terr.

HARRY STANLEY TAYLOR, '87. Law student. Willoughby, O.

LOREN ALONZO SADLER, '87. Hudson, O.

##### XLVI.

JOHN THADDEUS CARTER, '88. 1914 Walker street, Cleveland, O.

EDWARD PIERCE HALL, '88. Studying law Ashtabula, O.

THOMAS MARTIN KENNEDY, '88. 133 Lyman street, Cleveland, O.

JOHN FARIS BERRY, '88. Hudson, O.

EDWIN ALONZO CLARK, '87. Willoughby, O.

HENRY BURT HERRICK, '88. On bail nine. Chester Cross Roads, Geauga county, O.

STERLING PARKS, '88. Now at University of Michigan and member of Lambda. Collamer, O.

##### XLVII.

JULIAN DANA HARMON, '88. Warren, O.

CLAY HERRICK, '89. Collamer, O.

FRANCIS ANDERSON LYMAN, '89. Hilo, Hawaii, Sandwich Islands.

GEORGE ROBERT McKAY, '89. Now at Ada College. Newburg, O.

CLAIRE FRANK LUTHER, '89. Painesville, O.

## WESTMINSTER CHAPTER.

[The Alpha Delta, at Westminster College, Fulton, Mo.]

Westminster is the only Presbyterian college in Missouri. Both the northern and the southern branches of the church participate in the management. The institution was chartered in 1853. The college department has six professors and about ninety students. There is a preparatory department. Women are not admitted.

The only fraternities are Beta Theta Pi and Phi Delta Theta.

The Alpha Delta was founded in 1868. Since 1881 the corresponding secretaries have been J. R. Moorehead, A. A. Wallace, B. H. Charles, Jr., and W. R. Dobyns. Morehead has been chief of the district. The delegates at the convention of 1881 were J. G. Trimble, J. R. Moorehead, and H. C. Evans; at that of '82, J. R. Moorehead and E. B. M'Clure; at that of '84, B. H. Charles, Jr., W. R. Dobyns, and E. F. McCausland; and at that of '85, W. R. Dobyns, B. H. Charles, Jr., and F. W. Sneed.

### Admitted since August, 1881.

#### XLIII.

EDWIN FOUCHE McCAUSLAND, '86. Anniversary orator Philalethian Society in '85. Dardenne, Mo.

THOMAS TRAVIS TRIMBLE, '85. Student at Southwestern Presbyterian University. Home, Santa Fe, Mo.

#### XLIV.

WALTER HENSIL BRADLEY, '86. Anniversary orator Philalethian Society, '84; Dalton essay prize '85. Foley, Mo.

GEORGE DONELLAN, '87. Druggist. Independence, Mo.

#### XLV.

JOHN MOSBY GRANT, '86. Anniversary orator Philalethian Society '85; Harrison declamation prize, '84. Williamsburg, Mo.

LEROY JONES, '85. Anniversary orator Philalethian Society '84; student of medicine. Sedalia, Mo.

WILLIAM RAY DOBYNS, '87. Marquess oratorical prize '85; anniversary orator Philalethian Society '86; cor. sec. Austin, Tex.

FRANK WOODFORD SNEED, '87. Anniversary orator Philalethian Society, '83; Marquess prize for oratory '84. Sedalia, Mo.

#### XLVI.

WILLIAM HARRISON, JR., '88. Student in pharmacy. McCredie, Mo.

JOSEPH WILLIAM CHARLES, '87. Anniversary orator Philologic Society, '85. Fulton, Mo.

HUGH ALEXANDER ROBERTS, '88. Trimble Latin prize '84. St. Charles, Mo.

#### XLVII.

ROBERT LEE SIMPSON, '87. Anniversary orator Philalethian Society '86; cor. sec. Paris, Mo.

GEORGE RICHMOND MOULTON, '88. Foster mathematical prize '84; farmer. Independence, Mo.

CHARLES FRANCIS NESBITT, '88. Anniversary orator Philologic Society, '86. Washington, D. C.

HOWARD SUTHERLAND, '89. 2635 Chestnut street. St. Louis, Mo.

## UNIVERSITY OF WISCONSIN CHAPTER.

### [The Alpha Pi, at the University of Wisconsin, Madison, Wis.]

The University of Wisconsin is a state institution. In the undergraduate department there are thirty-three instructors and about four hundred students. Women are admitted. The studies are largely elective. Degrees are conferred in arts, letters, science, agriculture, and engineering. There is a law department, with seven instructors and about sixty students.

The fraternities are Phi Delta Theta, Beta Theta Pi, Phi Kappa Psi, Chi Psi, Sigma Chi, and Delta Upsilon.

The Alpha Pi was founded in 1872. Since the convention of 1881 the corresponding secretaries have been E. C. Stevens, E. G. McGilton, L. P. Conover, and H. S. Shedd. Conover was chief of the district. At the convention of 1881 the representatives were H. L. Smith, Stanley Proudfit, and J. M. Dodson: at that of 1882, E. C. Stevens, B. G. Treat, and L. P. Conover; at that of 1884, Conover; and at that of 1885, J. N. Sanborn. The chapter rarely has more than eight or nine members.

### Admitted since August, 1881.

#### XLIII.

EWING LAW PATTERSON, '82. From Pi. Terre Haute, Ind.

FREDERICK MASON BROWN, '85. Madison, Wis.

RUGGLES STARR ROCKWELL, '84. Columbus, Wis.

LAWRENCE PETERSON CONOVER, '85. Cor. sec. Dayton, O.

#### XLIV.

CHARLES ISAAC EARLL, '85. Whitewater, Wis.

HENRY PAXON STODDART, '83. Black Earth, Wis.

CONRAD MARTINIUS CONRADSON, '83. Brooklyn, Wis.

#### XLV.

RODELL CURTIS WARNE, '85. Whitewater, Wis.

FREDERICK AUGUSTUS TEALL, '85 law. Eau Claire, Wis.

FREDERICK MARMADUKE STEPHENSON, '85 law. Menominee, Wis.

#### XLVI.

CHARLES MARCIUS MORRIS, '87. Madison, Wis.

GEORGE LANGSTAFF THAYER, '87. Norwood Park, Cook county, Ill.

RUSSELL HUMPHREY SMITH, '87. Chicago, Ill.

HENRY SPRAGUE SHEDD, '86. Cor. sec. From Chi. Whitewater, Wis.

JOHN LAWRENCE MITLAND, '88. Markesan, Wis.

#### XLVII.

ALFRED PHELPS DELANCY, '87. Whitewater, Wis.

WINFIELD ROBERT SMITH, '89. Milwaukee, Wis.

FREDERICK WILLIAM STEARNS, '89. Madison, Wis.

#### XLVIII.

JACOB JOHN SCHINDLER, '89. Monroe, Wis.

SEYMOUR SHEPARD COOK. Special student. Whitewater, Wis.

## WITTENBERG CHAPTER.

### [The Alpha Gamma, at Wittenberg College, Springfield, O.]

Wittenberg College belongs to the Lutheran church. It comprises theological, collegiate, and preparatory departments. In the collegiate department there are six instructors and, including a few women, about one hundred students. Phi Kappa Psi, Beta Theta Pi, Alpha Tau Omega, and Phi Gamma Delta have chapters, with an average membership of twelve. The Alpha Gamma was established in 1867. Its corresponding secretaries since 1881 have been S. S. Kauffman, S. E. Greenawalt, II. A. Williams, C. J. Pretzman, F. L. Sigmund, and J. S. Simon. Greenawalt is chief of the district. R. II. Grube was at convention in 1881; S. S. Kauffman, E. P. Otis, and W. A. Pugh in 1882; and C. J. Pretzman and R. C. Bancroft in 1884.

#### Admitted since August, 1881.

#### XLIII.

CHARLES CLIFFORD PATTERSON, '84. Principal of High School. Bellefontaine, O.; former address, 228 West High street, Springfield, O.

ELLSWORTH OTIS, '87. Now at University of Michigan, studying law; member of Lambda, Winfield, O.

ARTHUR MERCEIN MANN, '85. Transferred to Theta. Clarksburg, O.

CHARLES JOHN PRETZMAN, '86. Cor. sec. 74 West High street, Springfield, O.

FRANK B. HEIBERTSHAUSEN, '86. Sulphur Springs, O.

HENRY ARCHER WILLIAMS, '85. First honor; editor College Stylus; cor. sec; studying law. 774 East Clifton street, Springfield, O.

EMOR W. SIMON, '84. Studying theology at Wittenberg Theological Seminary. New Lisbon, O.

ALLEN GARRETT BILLOW, '86. Ferncliff avenue, Springfield, O.

#### XLIV.

WILLIAM HARRISON KEPHART, '86. 1325 Seventh avenue, Altoona, Pa.

CARL KRIDER MOWER, '86. Factory street, Springfield, O.

FREDERICK LESTER SIGMUND, '86. Prize oration at junior exhibition; cor sec. Peabody, Kas.

#### XLV.

CALVIN LEWIS KNERR, '84. Dayton, O.

ELLSWORTH BROXELL KNERR, '84. Assistant instructor in sciences at Wittenberg College. Dayton, O.

WILLIAM ASBURY TOPE, '85. Studying medicine. New Philadelphia, O.

ROBERT CHRISTY BANCROFT, '87. Springfield, O.

JACOB SPENER SIMON, '87. Prize oration at junior exhibition; cor. sec. New Lisbon, O.

JOHN LAWRENCE MOORE. Treasurer I., B. & W. R'y. Sandusky, O.

#### XLVI.

ISAAC DOUGLASS WORMAN, '88. Leetonia,O.

ARTHUR HARMS SMITH, '88. Springfield, O.

EDWARD OSCAR WEAVER, '88. Springfield, O.

SAMUEL SMITH KELLER, '88. Springfield, O.

#### XLVII.

GAINS GLENN ATKINS, '88. Transferred to Theta Delta. Columbus, O.

WILLIAM A. BOWMAN, '89. Muncie, Ind.

HARRY HUMPHREYS, '89. Springfield, O.

## WOOSTER CHAPTER.

[The Alpha Lambda, at the University of Wooster, Wooster, O.]

The University of Wooster is a Presbyterian institution. In the collegiate department there are fourteen instructors and, including women, about two hundred and fifty students. Degrees are conferred in arts, philosophy, and literature. There is a large preparatory department.

There are chapters of Phi Kappa Psi, Beta Theta Pi, Phi Delta Theta, Sigma Chi, Delta Tau Delta, and Phi Gamma Delta. Membership averages fifteen.

The Alpha Lambda dates from 1872. Its corresponding secretaries since the convention of 1881 have been Jacob Brilles, J. S. Gooding, E. E. Weaver, Frank Burgoyne, and Frank Conrad. The representatives at recent conventions were, in 1881, J. H. McDonald, F. B. Pearson, and J. Cal. Hanna; in 1882, Hanna, D. S. Moore, and T. G. McConkey; in 1883, Jacob Brilles; in 1884, E. E. Weaver and Brilles, the latter being the secretary; and in 1885, J. Cal. Hanna. In 1882–'83 Hanna was chief of the district, and since 1884 he has been general secretary. In 1884–'85 Pearson was college secretary in the general secretary's department.

Admitted since August, 1881.

### XLIII.

Dickson Leonard Moore, '85. Second-honor man; editor of *Index* '84; captain in the university battalion; teaching. Present address, Farmersville, O.; home, Dayton, O.

Geo. Terry Dunlap, '86. Book-seller and stationer. Orrville, O.

Edward Ebenezer Weaver, '85. Fourth-honor man class '85; captain in university battalion; cor. sec.; book-keeper. Canton, O.

### XLIV.

Chas. Alvah Burrell, '86. Grocer. Huntington, O.

Geo. Albert Shives, '86. Wooster editor Mansfield *News*. Wooster, O.

Stanley Cass Archibald, '86. From Epsilon; out of college. Cincinnati, O.

George Howard Archibald, '86. Out of college. Wooster, O.

Edward Payson Dunlap, '87. *Index* editor '86. Orrville, O.

Samuel Kirkwood, '88. Now student at Macalaster College. St. Paul, Minn.

John McCoy, '84. Student at Princeton Theological Seminary. Chillicothe, O.

Delano Franklin Conrad, '87. Cor. sec. Princeton, Ind.

### XLV.

James Harrington Boyd, '86. Student at Princeton. Home, Keene, O.

Jas. Cavalier Conway, '85. Teacher. Present address, South Charleston, O.; permanent, Catawba, O.

Wm. Paul Kirkwood, '89. Student at Macalaster College. St. Paul, Minn.

Arthur Beardsley Dunlap, '87. Greenfield, O.

Frank Ward Burgoyne, '86. Editor *University Voice*; cor. sec. Cincinnati, O.

Wm. Warren Barnett, '87. Clerk. Dayton, O.

Geo. Dunlap Crothers, '87. Teacher. Present address, Eagle Pass, Tex.; permanent address, Greenfield, O.

Llewellyn Bodman Reakirt, '88. Clerk. Cincinnati, O.

Daniel Edward Jenkins, '87. Student at Melbourne University. Melbourne, Australia.

### XLVI.

Frank William Hoe, '87. Grocer. West Jefferson, O.

Geo. Homer Billman, '87. Captain university battalion. Akron, O.

Josiah Madison Estep, '88. Student Rensselaer Polytechnic Institute. Troy, N. Y.; Cadiz, O.

Wm. Henry Hauser, '88. Printer. Cadiz, O.

### XLVII.

Jacob Newton Brown, '88. Student at Miami University. Cincinnati, O.

Alexander Frank Keener, '87. Indiana, Pa.

John Maitland Macdonald, '89. Clerk. Cincinnati, O.

Jerome Kirke Smith, '89. Wooster, O.

Wm. O. Barnitz, '89. Student at Tarrytown Military Academy. Middletown, O.

Thos. Spencer Dunlap, '89. Orrville, O.

George A. Nesbitt, '89. Oxford, O.

John F. Hughes, '89. Parisville, O.

Chas. McClellan Moderwell, '89. Geneseo, Ill.

Frank Elmer Bradshaw, '87. Brookfield, Mo.

Thos. Parker Berry, '88. Barnesville, O.

### XLVIII.

Ferdinand Schwill, '89. Cincinnati, O.

.

# GEOGRAPHICAL INDEX TO THE YOUNGER MEMBERS.

[N. B.—In this index it will be noticed that some names appear more than once. The explanation is that some persons have, besides their principal address, a subordinate address; for example, their former home or the place where they are now studying. Subordinate addresses are designated by inclosing names in parentheses. The college addresses of active members are not given here, but appear in the chapter lists.]

## ALABAMA.

Anniston
  J H Noble          Cum
Athens
  Broussa's Coman    Cum
Birmingham
  G B Ward           Cum

Carthage
  C F Woods          Va
Demopolis
  N R Clarke         Va
Mobile
  C A Hall           Ste

Montgomery
  H B Everhart       Ste
  B J Fitzpatrick    Va
Selma
  Nathan Waller      Cum

## ARKANSAS.

Morrillton
  C C Barrows        Van

Vandale
  O N Killough       Miss

Washington
  A H Carrigan, Jr   Cum

## CALIFORNIA.

Berkeley
  A D Schindler      Cali
  Whitney Palache    Cali
  J C Doonin         Cali
  W I Kip            Cali
Durham
  C H Forbes         Mich
East Oakland
  R T Stratton       Cali
Fruitvale
  W B Weilman        Cali
Haywards
  E S Warren         Cali
Hopland
  A J Thatcher       Cali

Los Angeles
  A H Pratt          Am
  C W Barnes         Cali
  H L Shively        Cor
  M G Eshman         Ind
Napa City
  J E Beard          Cali
  H F Briggs         Nev
Nevada City
  W H Wentworth      Cali
Niles
  O B Ellsworth      Cali
Oakland
  E D Hale           Am
  R C Turner         Cali
  F C Turner         Cali

  G M Stratton       Cali
  C J Evans          Cali
  Hugh Howell        Cali
San Francisco
  J W Dutton         Cali
  R B Hellman        Cali
  J F Davis          Cali
  Gaillard Stoner    Cali
  Finlay Cook        Cali
  A R Baum           Harv
  H E Wise           Ind
San Rafael
  G W Dutton         Cali
Santa Cruz
  W S Iliff          Nw

## COLORADO.

Canon City
  Olin Templin       Kas
Colorado Springs
  N M Campbell       Ia
Denver
  C H Doolittle      Col
  E E Kitchen        Den
  G W Robinson       Kas

  G C Manly          Mich and Nw
  W A Moore          Nw
  A T Moore          Nw
  (W J Cady          Nw)
  C S Manly          O W
Georgetown
  C J White          Nw

Greeley
  A C Patton         Ind
South Pueblo
  W F Hamp           Cor
Trinidad
  R E L Holmes       Va

## CONNECTICUT.

Bridgeport
  C L Libby    Me
Buckingham
  H D J Gardner    Am
Chaplin
  (C J Backus    Am)
Cromwell
  (Dr W L Savage Am)
Ellington
  (E A Aborn    Am)

Hartford
  (G W Reed    Am)
  (A J Dyer    Am)
  (H D J Gardner   Am)
Middletown
  (H T Fernald    Me)
  (G W Barhydt    Un)
New Haven
  (G R Dickinson Am)

  (G F Prentiss    Am)
  (E R Tillinghast Nw)
  (E G Coldewey Ste)
Newington
  (T C Elliott    Am)
Summers
  F R Percival    Cor
Waterbury
  E F Lewis    Ste

## DAKOTA.

Blunt
  Henry Hamill    Nw

Grand Forks
  W A Gordon    Am
  J E Dike    Me

## DELAWARE.

Dover
  (Dr T B Bradford Pa)

Wilmington
  W L Cooling    Cor

## DISTRICT OF COLUMBIA.

Washington
  W T Partridge    Col
  W P Cutler    Cor
  J H Drown    Cor

  H P Mozier    Ia
  William Morey,Jr. Me
  C E Powell
    Mich and Van

  M L Shackelford RM
  C F Nesbitt    Westm

## FLORIDA.

Eufaula
  Dr H L Brannon Van

McMeekin
  E H Bowser    Van

Seffner
  M G Park    OW

## GEORGIA.

Atlanta
  C D Roy    Rich
La Grange
  H R Slack, Jr    JH

Louisville
  Wright Hunter    Van
Macon
  C A Caldwell    Van

## ILLINOIS.

Alvin
  Howard McElroy DP
Anna
  Samuel Dodds    Rut
Ashton
  J E Hunt    Nw
Aurora
  E C Quereau    Nw
Batavia
  W J Brown    Bel
Bloomington
  (W R Goodwin DP)
  E B Lanier    Nw

Bradford
  J A Lyman    Bel
Cerro Gordo
  J P Reasoner    DP
Cherry Valley
  F H Chase    Bel
  G A Chase    Bel
Chicago
  W E Hinchliff    Am
  L H McCormick Am
  D L Gifford    Am
  J R Montgomery Bel
  S O Dauchy    Bel

  A H Armstrong Bel
  S T Hickman    Cen
  T W Tomlinson Cor
  W R Goodwin DP
  F W Tilden    Harv
  W S Harwood    Ia
  (G S Cox    Ken)
  C L Andrews    Mich
  (W E Davidson Nw)
  A R Edwards    Nw
  C N Zeublin    Nw
  R H Smith
    Ste and Wis

## ILLINOIS—CONTINUED.

| | | |
|---|---|---|
| **Danville** | | |
| L P Cain | Wab | |
| **Dwight** | | |
| J P McWilliams | New | |
| **Elgin** | | |
| J B Young | Nw | |
| **Elmwood** | | |
| J T Lees | WR | |
| **Englewood** | | |
| Louis Rich | Nw | |
| **Evanston** | | |
| E P Vandercook | Am | |
| W O Shepherd | DP | |
| F E Miller | Nw | |
| H R Hatfield | Nw | |
| Bond Stowe | Nw | |
| C G Lewis | Nw | |
| Harvey Brown | Nw | |
| J B Hubbard | Nw | |
| H R Calkins | Nw | |
| P E Shumway | Nw | |
| F C Whitehead | Nw | |
| **Farmer City** | | |
| C M Weedman | Nw | |
| **Freeport** | | |
| H M Hyde | Bel | |

| | | |
|---|---|---|
| **Galesburg** | | |
| G L Price | Mich | |
| **Geneseo** | | |
| C M Moderwell | Woos | |
| **Hillsboro** | | |
| (J P Whitehead | Am) | |
| **Homewood** | | |
| A C Egelston | Un | |
| **Hyde Park** | | |
| H C Brown | Bel | |
| **Lafayette** | | |
| W E Davidson | Nw | |
| **Lake Forest** | | |
| E A Aborn | Am | |
| **Lincoln** | | |
| E C Randolph | OW | |
| **Mendota** | | |
| (D L Gifford | Am) | |
| **Norwood Park** | | |
| G L Thayer | Wis | |
| **Ottawa** | | |
| G B Penney | Cor | |
| (W D Fullerton | Nw) | |
| **Paris** | | |
| J W Doak | Wab | |

| | | |
|---|---|---|
| **Pekin** | | |
| W T Smith | | IaW and Mich |
| F L Toennigs | IaW | |
| E F Smith | IaW | |
| O H Unland | IaW | |
| F L Velde | Mich | |
| **Peoria** | | |
| G H Gibson | Cor | |
| **Rantoul** | | |
| A P Gulick | DP | |
| J L Benedict | DP | |
| C P Benedict | DP | |
| **Rockford** | | |
| J R Robertson | Bel | |
| S M Bushnell | Bel | |
| H H Hamilton | Mad | |
| J W Gregory | Mich | |
| **Rossville** | | |
| (Howard McElroy DP) | | |
| **Van Orin** | | |
| W E Wood | Mich | |
| **Yorkville** | | |
| John Adams | Nw | |

## INDIANA.

| | | |
|---|---|---|
| **Battle Ground** | | |
| J G Campbell | DP | |
| **Bedford** | | |
| J F Thornton | Ind | |
| **Bloomington** | | |
| F H Hughes | Ind | |
| Albert Miller | Ind | |
| R F Hight | Ind | |
| B V Sudbury | Ind | |
| C R Madison | Ind | |
| **Burlington** | | |
| D P Grant | Mich | |
| **Cloverdale** | | |
| E E Mullinix | Ind | |
| O E Mullinix | Ind | |
| **Columbus** | | |
| Herman Carr | Ind | |
| **Crawfordsville** | | |
| M H Insley | Wab | |
| S A Trout | Wab | |
| Harry Greene | Wab | |
| A A McCain | Wab | |
| J A Greene | Wab | |
| **Cutler** | | |
| Walter Wyatt | Ind | |

| | | |
|---|---|---|
| **Economy** | | |
| C H Oler | Ind | |
| **Evansville** | | |
| Arthur Thayer | DP | |
| C E Johnson | Va | |
| F W Cook, Jr | Wab | |
| **Gosport** | | |
| W H Galloway | Ind | |
| **Greencastle** | | |
| W S Scott | DP | |
| G H Murphy | DP | |
| I J Hammond | DP | |
| **Greensburg** | | |
| J W Rucker | DP | |
| L E Lathrop | DP | |
| Clarence Cumback | | |
| deceased | DP | |
| F M Walters | Ind | |
| C M Cunningham | Ind | |
| J S Shannon | Ind | |
| **Green's Fork** | | |
| N L Bunnell | Ind | |
| **Guilford** | | |
| J B Robertson | Van | |
| **Hanover** | | |
| J C Clemmons | Han | |

| | | |
|---|---|---|
| **Huntington** | | |
| F J Bippus | Wab | |
| **Indianapolis** | | |
| W E Bryce | Cen | |
| W C Smith | DP | |
| Harry Bowser | DP | |
| J W Wharton | Ind | |
| J H Howard | Ind | |
| H R Hess | Wab | |
| **Knightsville** | | |
| C M Zellar | DP | |
| **Laconia** | | |
| R F Evans | Han | |
| **Lafayette** | | |
| J W Kieff | Wab | |
| **Lebanon** | | |
| W H Masters | DP | |
| **Logansport** | | |
| E B McConnell | Cor | |
| (T W Tomlinson Cor) | | |
| **Madison** | | |
| R M Dillon | Han | |
| **Moorefield** | | |
| (S M Rutherford DP) | | |
| **Muncie** | | |
| W A Bowman | Wit | |

## INDIANA—Continued.

## INDIAN TERRITORY.

## IOWA.

## KANSAS.

## KANSAS—Continued.

**Emporia**
Edwin Fowler        Am
T C Elliott         Am
**Garden City**
W W Davis           Kas
J H Cotteral        Mich
**Garnett**
T W Houston         Kas
**Hutchinson**
C E Hall            Kas
**Lawrence**
C E Parker
    Col. Kas, and Mich
O H Pochler         Kas
R C Rankin          Kas
C D Dean            Kas
E F Stimpson        Kas
Harry Bucking-
    ham             Kas
J B Lippincott      Kas
**Lyons**
W E Borah           Kas

**McPherson**
M N Breman          Kas
**Manhattan**
(I B Todd           Ken)
**Meade Centre**
W S Kinnear         Kas
**Newton**
A N Loper           Ia
F E Reed            Kas
W T Reed            Kas
**Nortonville**
J E Curry           Kas
**Ottowa**
(C E Parker
    Col. Kas, and Mich)
**Peabody**
F L Sigmund         Wit
**Shawnee**
Archibald Watson    Kas
C M Watson          Kas
G B Watson          Mich

**Spring Hill**
G B Deem            Nw
**Topeka**
F W Phelps          Am
Rev F B Vrooman     Bel
W H Davies          Den
H L Call            Kas
John Weightman      Kas
**Troy**
Warren Perry        Kas
**Vining**
W T Caywood         Kas
**Wamego**
C E Word            Kas
**Washington**
Rev C P P Fox       Mad
**Wellington**
H J Bone            Cum
H F Smith           Kas
**Winsfield**
W M Tomlin          Kas

## KENTUCKY.

**Antioch Mills**
(L C Woolery        Beth)
**Bedford**
J R Rowlett         Han
**Burlington**
William Gaines      SL
**Carrollton**
Smith O'Neal        Han
T R Bridges         Han
**Cloverport**
O T Skillman        Cen
E F Vest            Cen
**Covington**
E J Buffington      Van
**Danville**
W H Briggs          Cen
H L Briggs          Cen
C H Irvine          Cen
J W Guest, Jr       Cen
O B Caldwell        Cen
J W Caldwell        Cum
A C Downs           Mich
F J Cheek           Mich
(Dr Cornelius
    Skinner         Va)
**Elizabethtown**
W A Pusey           Van
A B Pusey           Van
**Frankfort**
I B Todd            Ken

**Fulton**
B C Mickle          Cum
**Glasgow**
E M Benedict        Ken
J B Ellis           Van
**Henderson**
Rev W D Blair       Cum
**Hopkinsville**
B S Radford         Cum
(C C Slaughter      Van)
C C Ferrell         Van
**Lawrenceburg**
R H Lillard         Beth
**Lexington**
F P St Clair        Beth
J H Kastle          JH
**Louisville**
S C Jones           Cen
S J Hayden          Cen
W S Mullen          Cen
R A Watts           Cen
Rev W B Riley       Han
(O B Riley          Han)
D A Walton          Ste
E G Coldewey        Ste
E M Drummond        Ste
J A Altsheler       Van
R F Hibbitt         Van
Dr Cornelius Skin-
    ner             Va

**Marion**
Lee Cruce           Van
**Marrowbone**
S R Pace            Cum
Rev J R Crawford    Cum
**Maysville**
W B Mathews, Jr.    Cen
Clarence Mathews    Cen
William Cochran     Cen
Jamie Cochran       Cen
**Mt Sterling**
J C Reid            Beth
H R Bright          Beth
G W Broadus         Cen
**New Liberty**
O B Riley           Han
W L Riley           Han
**Owensboro**
A Y Ford            Br
**Owenton**
J W L Slaughter     Van
**Paducah**
Linn White          Van
**Petersburg**
W T Crisler         SL
**Russellville**
A B Freeman         Cum
**Shelby City**
R G Denny           Cen

## KENTUCKY—Continued.

Smithysgrove
    J W Beck    Cum
Springfield
    C A Green    Cum

Stanford
    J S Owsley, Jr    Cum
Versailles
    J C Coleman    Cen
    C A McDonald    Van

    J A Guthrie    Van
    D T Edwards    Va
    W F McLeod    Va
Winchester
    J W McClure    Van

## LOUISIANA.

New Orleans
    H H Swain    Bel
    E L Lashbrooke    Miss

Shreveport
    L R Hamberlin    Rich

## MAINE.

Augusta
    J R Boardman    Me
    F L Thompson    Me
Bangor
    G N Jones    Harv
    C S Lunt    Me
    R K Jones, Jr    Me
    E C Vose    Me
    L G Paine    Me
    J K Chamberlin    Me
    L G Paine    Ste
Belfast
    F W Dickerson    Me
Bethel
    William Philbrook    Me
Bradley
    R H Marsh    Me

Brewer
    J F Lockwood    Me
    W H Sargent    Me
Dennysville
    H F Lincoln    Me
Enfield
    S S Twombly    Me
Harrington
    I B Ray    Me
    E V Collin    Me
    A J Collin    Me
North Bridgeton
    C G Cushman    Me
Orono
    H T Fernald    Me
    E D Graves    Me

    E C Bartlett    Me
    F T Drew    Me
Palermo
    G F Black    Me
Paris
    A E Forbes    SL
Portland
    C S Williams    Me
Rockland
    J D Lazell    Me
Skowhegan
    D W Colby    Me
Warren
    F E Hall    Me
West Summer
    H A Abbott    SL

## MARYLAND.

Baltimore
    J U Detrick    Dick
    C H Hammond    HS
    Louis Garthe    JH
    J D Lord    JH
    W S Bayley    JH
    W B Harlan    JH
    H W Williams    JH
    H H Wiegand    JH
    Theodore Hough    JH
    A R L Dohme    JH
    J R Winslow    JH

    W F Smith    JH
    C E Simon    JH
    W H Miller    JH
    E C Applegarth    JH
    Rollin Norris    Ste
    H L Gannt    Ste
Churchville
    (W B Harlan    JH)
Hagerstown
    C E Bikle    Dick
    (F T Baker    Dick)

Ilchester
    (Rollin Norris    Ste)
Mt Washington
    A T Collins    JH
Poolesville
    John White, Jr    JH
Snow Hill
    J R Todd    Dick
Tompkinsville
    G W C Smoot    Dick
Towson
    R M Isaac    Ste

## MASSACHUSETTS.

Amherst
    J H Tufts    Am
    (E B Woodin    Am)
    H P Woodin    Am
    C H White    Am
Andover
    (W P Taylor    Bos)

Auburndale
    J G Cramer    Bos
Beverly
    L H Wardwell    Bos
    (A D Cole    JH)
Boston
    (W S Boardman    Am)

    F H Fitts    Am
    R M Palmer    Am
    W B Snow    Bos
    Bernhard Berenson    Bos
    W S Little    Bos
    A P Folwell    Br

## MASSACHUSETTS—Continued.

| | | | | | | | |
|---|---|---|---|---|---|---|---|
| F H Briggs | Br | Granby | | Provincetown | |
| Guy Wilkinson | Cali | E W Branch | Bos | (1 F Smith | Am) |
| (H M Carter | Den) | Haverhill | | Raynham | |
| W M McInnes | Harv | (C E O Nichols | Am) | (C H White | Am) |
| E E Blodgett | Harv | Holbrook | | Rockland | |
| D B Brace | JH | G C Dean | Am | W H Poole | Am |
| C L Holmes | Me | Holyoke | | Salem | |
| H M Smith | SL | W F Whiting | Am | F P Ingalls | Cor |
| Buckland | | Hopedale | | Shelburne Falls | |
| (W D Forbes | Am) | G N Goddard | Am | W D Forbes | Am |
| Cambridge | | Lexington | | Somerville | |
| R D Wilson | Harv | G C Goodwin | Am | G E Whitaker | Bos |
| Cambridgeport | | Marblehead | | H T Allen | Harv |
| W M Warren | Bos | A E Knapp | Mad | South Gardner | |
| Campello | | Melrose | | H A Whitney | Am |
| W R Pattangall | Me | W H Williams | Harv | Springfield | |
| Chelsea | | Middleboro | | J E Tower | Am |
| F C Hood | Harv | A H Washburn | Cor | Stoneham | |
| Chicopee | | Monson | | (W B Snow | Bos) |
| Thomas Whiteside | Bos | (J H Tufts | Am) | Sudbury | |
| Cummington | | R H Cushman | Am | W H Thompson | Am |
| A J Dyer | Am | Newburyport | | Taunton | |
| Dorchester | | W S Boardman | Am | A E Wilbar | Am |
| E A Johnston | Bos | E S Drown | Harv | C B Wilbar | Am |
| East Boston | | North Adams | | W C Hawkins | Ste |
| L N Cushman | Bos | H C Lyman | Mad | Walpole | |
| East Marshfield | | Northampton | | (F H Fitts | Am) |
| J C Hagen | Bos | A F Stone | Am | Wellesley | |
| C R Richards | Bos | North Brookfield | | (W S Little | Bos) |
| Erving | | (J E Tower | Am) | West Newton | |
| (F W Phelps | Am) | H A Cooke | Am | Rev J C Jaynes | Harv |
| C D Phelps | Am | Palmer | | Winchester | |
| Everett | | S S Parks | Am | H C Holt | Harv |
| L B Greenwood | Bos | Pittsfield | | Worcester | |
| Framingham | | G W Reed | Am | C B Stevens | Am |
| (G P Eastman | Am) | C A Washburn | WR | J E Smith | Am |
| Gardner | | Plymouth | | (G E Whitaker | Bos) |
| G A Dunn | Bos | E S Damon | Am | | |

## MICHIGAN.

| | | | | | |
|---|---|---|---|---|---|
| Adrian | | Emery | | F R Babcock | Mich |
| H T Stephens | OS | D H Ramsdell | Mich | R S Babcock | Mich |
| Brighton | | Grand Ledge | | Niles | |
| L B Lee | Mich | R D Briggs | Mad | J H Bickford | D P |
| J H Lee | Mich | Grand Rapids | | Owosso | |
| Coldwater | | F D Sherman | Mich | J C Shattuck | Mich |
| F B Spaulding | Mich | Highland | | Pontiac | |
| Detroit | | W A St John | Mad | W C Harris | Mich |
| F T Lodge | DP | Lake Linden | | J H Patterson | Mich |
| M R Nelson | Mad | W W Harris, | | Shelby | |
| Dowagiac | | deceased, | Mich | W J Cady | Nov |
| V M Tuthill | Mich | Manistee | | | |
| | | D P Cochrane | Mich | | |

## MINNESOTA.

Clear Lake
    O W Baldwin     Col
Fort Snelling
    W D Howe     Ind
Minneapolis
    E M Stevens     Am

St Paul
    C J Backus     Am
    H H Cleveland     Col
    F A Bristol     Col
    D W Brownell     Den
    Julian Millard     Mich
    Dr G A Renz     Pa

Lewis Baker, Jr     Ste
M H Albin     Va
Samuel Kirkwood Woos
W P Kirkwood     Woos
Winona
    L R Doud     Mich

## MISSISSIPPI.

Ashland
    Hon W T Mc
      Donald     Miss
Atlanta
    A M Harley     Miss
Brandon
    Hon W H Clarke Cum
    H R Cocke     Miss
    Dr J J Rhodes     Miss
    E E Frantz     Miss
    A E Brown     Miss
    R L McLaurin     Miss
Brookhaven
    J S Gadberry     Miss
    J H Johnson     Miss
Coffeeville
    Hon Willis Golli-
      day     Cum
Columbia
    R P Moore     Miss
    T B Lampton     Miss
Columbus
    A L Pittman     Miss
    (J B McElroy     Miss)
Coma
    D L Heath     Va

Edwards
    T A Chichester     Miss
Hazlehurst
    W W Mayes     Miss
    R B Mayes     Miss
Holly Springs
    G R Craft     Cen
Jackson
    J B Ross     Miss
    W R Hill     Miss
Lexington
    A W Hooker
      Miss and Rich
Macon
    H E Harlan     Van
McComb City
    H M Quin     Miss
    H C Hoover     Miss
Mayhew Station
    J B McElroy     Miss
Meridian
    T W Scarborough Am
    R F Cochran     Miss
    J B Cochran     Miss
Natchez
    L K Sharpe     Miss

T S Sharpe     Miss
M C Montgomery Miss
A B Learned
      Miss and Van
Oxford
    G T Fitzhugh     Miss
    Rev W I Sinnott Miss
    L T Fitzhugh     Miss
    J D Burge     Miss
    S S Mathews     Miss
    Samuel Holloway Miss
Ripley
    J C Harris     Cum
    J Y Murry, Jr     Miss
    Walter Harris     Miss
Rosedale
    F M Scott     Miss
Tremont
    O T Stone     Cum
Tupelo
    O L Stribling     Cum
Vaden
    E W Stewart     Cum
West Point
    E L B McClelland Miss

## MISSOURI.

Brookfield
    F E Bradshaw     Woos
Clinton
    J E Atkinson     Beth
Dardenne
    E F McCausland Westm
Foley
    W H Bradley     Westm
Franklin
    N W Bonham     Van
Fulton
    J W Charles     Westm
Independence
    George Donellan Westm
    G R Moulton     Westm
Kansas City
    Frank Warriner     Beth

    J W Branmam     Cum
    Garrett Ellison     Den
    F G Graham     Dick
    R E Stout     Kas
    J A Sargent     Kas
    Carl Smith     Kas
    J G Smith     Mich
McCredie
    Wm Harrison, Jr Westm
Maryville
    B L C Gann     LaW
Memphis
    W B McArthur     OW
Paris
    R L Simpson     Westm
Pilot Grove
    W L McCutchen Cum
Rosendale
    J W Laney     LaW

St Charles
    Walter Alexander Harv
    H A Roberts     Westm
St Louis
    S D Roser     Cen
    Lee Dunlap     Cen
    C W Niedring-
      haus, dec'd,     DP
    Howard Suther-
      land     Westm
Santa Fe
    T T Trimble     Westm
Sedalia
    Leroy Jones     Westm
    F W Sneed     Westm
Williamsburg
    J M Grant     Westm

## MONTANA.

Deer Lodge
Howard Copland Den

Helena
W E Sanders Col

## NEBRASKA.

Kearney
J C Fifield Jll
Norfolk
A S Burrows Ia

Omaha
Dr W P Wilcox Col
V E Tucker Han
M C Hamilton Ste

## NEVADA.

Virginia City
M W Fredrick Harv

## NEW HAMPSHIRE.

New Hampton
(C O Williams Br)

Winchester
(W S Buffum Am)

## NEW JERSEY.

Bergen Point
E F White Ste
Bordentown
J B Reynolds Rut
Dover
J L Hurd Col
East Millstone
F W Ribble Rut
H L Rupert Rut
Glen Ridge
H G Darwin Col
Hoboken
F W Sheldon Cor
J H Sheldon Ste
Irvington
A B Harrison Rut

Jersey City
O E Coles Col
Jersey City Heights
W C Post Ste
Mt Holly
F T Baker Dick
W A Barrows, Jr Rut
Newark
C A Cahoone Col
W J Moore Mad
O H Baldwin Ste
North Plainfield
D C Adams Col
Paterson
W O Barnes Ste
Princeton
(G W Hutchinson Br)

(W H Robinson Un)
(John McCoy Woos)
(J H Boyd Woos)
Raritan
A W Mack Ste
L C Mack Ste
Seabright
W G Lake Dick
South Dennis
L A Parsels Dick
Summit
T S Fearn Jll
Verona
C W Harrison Rut
Windsor
G W Hutchinson Br

## NEW YORK.

Albany
(C W De Baun Un)
Amsterdam
F D Lewis Un
Antwerp
Theodore Miller Cor
Aurora
S C Jones Cor
Ballston Spa
N D Fish Un
R H Washburne Un
Bayonne
Rev J K Folwell Mad

Bellona
Thomas Carmody,
Jr., Cor
Binghamton
P J Casey, dec'd, Cor
W M Harris Cor
Bombay
J L Southwick Cor
Broadalbin
Rev W J Quincy Mad
N J Gulick Un
Brooklyn
Dr W L Savage Am

Jas Chambers, Jr Am
(A P Folwell Br)
W B Middleton Col
C F Ackerman Col
E H Barnum Col
J T Sackett Cor
J B Alden Rut
G B Helmle SL
C J Field Ste
Buffalo
G P Eastman Am
Rev C G Brelos Beth
J J Aspinwall Cor

## NEW YORK—Continued.

## NEW YORK—CONTINUED.

Valatie
  F H Silvernail   Un
Victor
  M F Webster   Cor
Walton
  C C Pierce   Mad
Wappinger's Falls
  F W Hargreaves  Cor

Warwick
  A B Bishop   Un
Waverley
  Rev D H Cooper Mad
West Hebron
  W H Robinson  Un
West Pierrepont
  J W Rafferty   SL

West Point
  (C B Hagadorne  Cor)
  (Arthur Thayer  DP)
  (W E Wood   Mich)
Whitney's Point
  (C M Baker  SL)
  F Y Adams   SL
Woodville
  F A Converse  Cor

## NORTH CAROLINA.

Asheville
  A M Carroll  Rich
Chapel Hill
  (J L Love   JH)

Gastonia
  J L Love   JH
Murfreesboro
  Percy Rowe  RM

Raleigh
  E B Smedes  JH

## OHIO.

Akron
  H L Jacobs  Am
  C B Raymond  Am
  K B Conger  Ken
  F M Raymund  OS
  G H Billman  Woos
Alexandria
  E H Castle  Den
  W E Castle  Den
Ashtabula
  E P Hall  WR
Athens
  C H Higgins  OU
  H R McVay  OU
Barnesville
  T P Berry  Woos
Beallsville
  F S Israel  Beth
Bellaire
  J A H Mertz  Beth
Bellefontaine
  C C Patterson  Wit
Bethesda
  A L White  Beth
Beverly
  H H Rumble  Beth
Bridgeport
  W H Wolf  Beth
Bucyrus
  (W C Sheppard  Den)
Cadiz
  J M Estep  Woos
  W H Hauser  Woos
Canton
  G E Cook  Ste
  E E Weaver  Woos

Catawba
  (J C Conway  Woos)
Chester Cross Roads
  H B Herrick  WR
Chillicothe
  (G C Manly
    Mich and Nw)
  John McCoy  Woos
Cincinnati
  J V B Scarborough Am
  W W Scarborough Am
  (T W Scarborough
    Am)
  J H McKenzie  Ros
  S C Archibald
    Cen and Woos
  T B Evans  Col
  Alfred Gaither  Harv
  Clinton Collins  Harv
  (M A Mayo  Ken)
  (E M Benedict  Ken)
  C K Benedict  Ken
  W D Fullerton  Nw
  E M Cranston  Nw
  (W R Pomerene OS)
  (C W DeLamatre OS)
  Julius Floto  OS
  T R Terwilliger  OW)
  (C C Pickering  OW)
  (T G Smith, Jr  Ste)
  (J W McClure  Van)
  F W Bargoyne  Woos
  L B Reakirt  Woos
  J N Brown  Woos
  J M Macdonald  Woos
  Ferdinand Schwill Woos

Clarksburg
  (A M Mann
    OW and Wit)
Cleveland
  Alexander Mc-
    Kinney  Beth
  G F Saal  Cor
  H C Ferris
    Ken and Ste
  H N Hill  Ken
  (Henry Abbey  Ste)
  J T Carter  WR
  T M Kennedy  WR
Collamer
  Sterling Parks
    Mich and WR
  Clay Herrick  WR
Columbus
  C V Pleukharp  OS
  W H Siebe t  OS
  W C Sabine  OS
  G G Atkins OS and Wit
  C A Doe  OW
  (M L Milligan  OW)
Coolville
  H H Humphrey  Cor
  Calvin Humphrey OU
Coshocton
  W R Pomerene  OS
Crestline
  R B Wyukoop  Ken
Dayton
  E C Benedict  OS
  L P Conover  Wis
  C L Knerr  Wit
  (E B Knerr  Wit)

## OHIO—Continued.

## OHIO—Continued.

Sandusky
  D J Mackey
          Mich and OS
  J L Moore          WN
Shelby
  W B Lowe          Beth
  H R Brown          Beth
South Charleston
  J C Conway          Woos
Springfield
  (C C Patterson     Wit)
  C J Pretzman       Wit
  H A Williams       Wit
  A G Billow          Wit
  C K Mower          Wit
  E B Knerr          Wit
  R C Bancroft       Wit
  A H Smith          Wit
  E O Weaver          Wit
  S S Keller          Wit
  Harry Humphreys Wit
Steubenville
  H L L Webb         OW

Sulphur Springs
  F B Heibertshausen Wit
Tappan
  L G Worstell        OU
Tiffin
  F T Pennington
              DP and OW
Tiltonville
  W W Medill          WJ
Toledo
  C L Curtis          Cor
  J L Wilkin          Den
Trimble
  J M Johnson         OU
Uhrichsville
  G W Reed          OU
Warren
  J D Harmon          WR
West Jefferson
  Gorman Jones        Den
  F W Hoe            Woos

West Middleburg
  E L Shannon         OW
Westville
  D H Sowers          OW
Willoughby
  N C Stevens         Harv
  Solon Loner         WR
  H S Taylor          WR
  E A Clark          WR
Winfield
  Ellsworth Otis      Wit
Winton Place
  B A Williams        OW
Wooster
  G A Shives          Woos
  G H Archibald       Woos
  J K Smith          Woos
Xenia
  E E Paine          OS
  (E L Shannon        OW)
Youngstown
  A M Dyer          Mad

## OREGON.

Salem
  Rev M L Rugg  Mad

Union
  J P Atkinson    Cum

## PENNSYLVANIA.

Alleghany City
  G W Willis          Br
Altoona
  W H Kephart         Wit
Belleville
  O M Campbell       WJ
Bentleysville
  (Dr F M Stephens Pa)
Bethlehem
  (G F Pettinos      Dick)
Burgettstown
  W J Fredericks      WJ
Carlisle
  G F Pettinos       Dick
Carmon
  J D Jack           WJ
Chester
  (G W Quick         Rich)
Easton
  (G F Saudt          Ste)
  F W Shick          Un
Everett
  A D Yocum          Dick
Greensburg
  F J Kimball         Me

Harrisburg
  A E Meily          Dick
Indiana
  A F Keener          Woos
Laurelton
  Dr H H Lincoln     Pa
Marchand
  B A Brown          WJ
Meadville
  (Solon Loner        WR)
New Castle
  N A Philips         Beth
Newville
  W B Stewart         Dick
North Hope
  J F Reigart         Dick
Pennsville
  J D Atkinson        Ind
Philadelphia
  Louis Shiel, dec'd Br
  (R T Stratton      Cali)
  David Brown         Dick
  F M Welsh          Dick
  J C Reynolds        Dick

Maurice Fels          JH
  W H Crawshaw       Mad
  H G McKean         Mad
  (C R Dundore       Pa)
  H L Patterson       Pa
  W E Maison          Pa
  Dr T B Bradford    Pa
  H A Davis          Pa
  S E Scott, dec'd    Pa
  (Dr N P Grimm      Pa)
  Dr H A Hare         Pa
  Dr J M Bradford    Pa
  R S Maison          Pa
  Dr C J Irvin        Pa
  H P Ball           Pa
  F C Clarke          Pa
  Alfred Weeks, Jr Pa
  J P Krecker         Pa
  George Fetterolf   Pa
  G C Bowker          Pa
  G A Freyer          Pa
  T G Smith, Jr       Ste
Pittsburg
  C H Hirst          OS
  W R Cochrane       Pa

## PENNSYLVANIA—Continued.

Somerset
F M Kimmel    Beth
A J Colborn, Jr    Beth
Washington
J M Thompson    WJ

William McKen-
nan    WJ
R M Brownson    WJ
T R McKennan    WJ
M S McKennan    WJ

R T Jones    WJ
W A Baird    WJ
West Chester
Dr N P Grimm    Pa

## RHODE ISLAND.

Central Falls
J W Freeman    Br
Hope Valley
E R Tillinghast    Nw
Middletown
J H Ward    Br
Newport
H G Wood    Br

C E Lawton    Br
Providence
C P Seagrave    Br
A P Sumner    Br
C O Williams    Br
E E Pierce    Br
Norman Gunder-
son    Br

E T Banning    Br
H F Caldwell    Br
G H Crooker    Br
F J Belcher    Br
H L Cattannach    Br
H J Rhett    Br
R L Spencer    Br
A F Clark    Br

## SOUTH CAROLINA.

Darlington
J L Coker    Ste
Lawtonville
A M Bostick    Rich

Newberry
B B Ramage    Harv
J H McIntosh    JH

Spartanburg
J P Smith    Van
Williamston
J M Lawder    Van

## TENNESSEE.

Bakerville
J F Fowlkes    Cum
Bartlett
G W Blackwell    Van
Carthage
W E Myer    Van
Chattanooga
J C Guild    Van
W R Patten    Van
L S Merriam    Van
Clarksville
T T Trimble    Westm
Columbia
W C Whitthorne    Cen
H Y Whitthorne    Cen
A L Prewett    Van
Harpeth
J S Buchannan    Cum
Haw's Cross Roads
W H Epps    Cum
Henderson's Cross Roads.
R B Williams    Cum
Humboldt
S C Williams    Van
Jonesboro
J A Harris    Van

Hendrick's Creek
J C Ritter    Cum
Knoxville
H H Parker    Cum
Las Casas
W H Martin    Cum
Lebanon
C L McDonnold    Cum
Curry Kirkpatrick    Cum
I W P Buchanan    Cum
G B Kilpatrick    Cum
Memphis
C E Pate    Cum
J W Chalmers    Miss
R B Maury, Jr    Va
Milton
E E Sneed    Cum
Morristown
J L Summers    Van
Nashville
Dr J W Handley    Cum
H M Drifoos    Cum
C L Jungerman    Van
E W Thompson    Van
J H Kelley    Van
J J G Ruhm    Van

C C Slaughter    Van
A G Hall    Van
C W Beale    Van
C L Thornburg    Van
E B Davis    Van
W T Guild    Van
Alfred Hume    Van
Tyler Calhoun    Van
Granville Allison    Van
W C Brannum    Van
R D Goodlett, Jr    Van
W G Kirkpatrick    Van
New Middletown
F G Bridges    Cum
Ripley
A J Barbee    Van
Sparta
F A Gallup    Mad
Sweetwater
A S Dickey    Cum
Union City
R P Whitesell    Van
Winchester
A D Marks    Cum
Withe
R A Cody    Cum

## TEXAS.

| Austin | | |
| --- | --- | --- |
| Wendel Spence | Cum |
| W R Dobyns | Westm |
| Brownwood | | |
| Rev R W Lewis | Cum |
| N S Walker | Miss |
| Cuero | | |
| W J Baker | Cum |
| Da Villa | | |
| J H Miller | Cum |
| Eagle Pass | | |
| G D Crothers | Woos |
| Fort Worth | | |
| Hallett Harding | Cum |

| Gainesville | | |
| --- | --- | --- |
| H L Stuart | R M |
| Galveston | | |
| T S Lyon | Va |
| Gonzales | | |
| J T Atkinson | Va |
| Jefferson | | |
| W B Ward | Van |
| La Rissa | | |
| W P Bone | Cum |
| McKinney | | |
| J B Kerr | Cum |
| W T L Clark | Miss |

| Marshall | | |
| --- | --- | --- |
| E P Hill | Cum |
| A H Cooper | Cum |
| Salado | | |
| Rev J R Hodges | Cum |
| San Antonio | | |
| W B Houston | Cum |
| Sherman | | |
| W G Richardson | Miss |
| Weatherford | | |
| W T Watson | Cum |
| Winsborough | | |
| C M Templeton | Cum |

## VERMONT.

| Keeler's Bay | | |
| --- | --- | --- |
| F W Sears | Am |
| A P Smith | Am |
| Mechanicsville | | |
| B C Gillis | Bos |

| St Johnsbury | | |
| --- | --- | --- |
| (A F Stone | Am |
| Stowe | | |
| (E D Hale | Am) |
| Windham | | |
| G F Prentiss | Am |

## VIRGINIA.

| Aldie | | |
| --- | --- | --- |
| C L Laws | Rich |
| Ashland | | |
| (C T Patton | R M) |
| J L Patton | R M |
| R W Patton | R M |
| J J Leake | R M |
| Bentiooglio | | |
| A T Patton | Va |
| Blackstone | | |
| J P Epes | HS |
| Bowling Green | | |
| (Percy Rowe | R M) |
| Carlett P O | | |
| Dr L P Coates | Pa |
| Childsburg | | |
| C T Smith, Jr | Rich |
| Concord Depot | | |
| D S Evans, Jr | HS |
| Cross Keys | | |
| C C Hering | R M |
| Cuthbert | | |
| T P Branch | Van |
| Danville | | |
| T N Ferrell | Rich |
| W R Fitzgerald | Rich |
| Farmville | | |
| R E L Blanton | HS |
| Farmwell | | |
| G W Quick | Rich |
| Gordonsville | | |
| O J Wise, dec'd | Va |

| Hampden Sidney College | | |
| --- | --- | --- |
| W H Bocock | HS and Va |
| J D Eggleston, Jr | HS |
| W H Wilson | HS |
| A R Shaw | HS |
| Ivor | | |
| (R E L Holmes | Va) |
| Jamaica | | |
| A J Montague | Va |
| Jennings' Ordinary | | |
| W A Watson | HS |
| Little Plymouth | | |
| T J Bland | R M |
| Lynchburg | | |
| Robert Winfree | R M |
| H L Winfree | R M |
| J S Hobson | R M |
| P B Winfree | R M |
| W W Talley | Rich and Va |
| A W Terrell | Va |
| Mechum's River | | |
| Alfred Bagby, Jr | Rich |
| Mossy Creek | | |
| J B Finley | HS |
| Norfolk | | |
| J B Jenkins | Harv |
| Petersburg | | |
| (H R McIlwaine | HS) |
| M T Peed | JH |
| W H Perkinson | Va |

| Portsmouth | | |
| --- | --- | --- |
| J A Boram | Rich |
| F D Tabb | Rich |
| Pungoteague | | |
| O F Mears | R M |
| Richmond | | |
| G B Stacy | Beth |
| G T Patton | R M |
| (W W Talley | Rich and Va |
| W R Thomas | Rich |
| E B Pollard | Rich |
| H H Harris | Rich |
| L S Lyon | Rich |
| W E Tanner, Jr | Rich |
| Frank Lyon | Rich |
| R A Cutler | Rich |
| G B Stacy | Rich |
| R C Williams | Rich |
| A S J Dudley | Van |
| J R Tucker, Jr | Va |
| San Marino | | |
| T T Jones | HS |
| Stevensville | | |
| (Alfred Bagby, Jr | Rich) |
| White Post | | |
| J W Kern | Va |
| Winchester | | |
| M H Albin | Va |
| Yancey | | |
| W A Gibbons | R M |

# WASHINGTON TERRITORY.

Seattle
    Charles Jones    WR

Yakima
    Samuel Hubbard,
      Jr        Cali

## WEST VIRGINIA.

Bethany
    W K Pendleton,
      Jr       Beth
    L C Woolery    Beth

Charleston, Kanawha county
    F M Staunton    Cor
    C C Lewis, Jr    HS

Charlestown, Jefferson county
    W B Hopkins    HS
    A C Hopkins    HS
    J P Campbell    JH

Gerardstown
    H C V Campbell  HS

Huntington
    Garland Buffing-
      ton      RM
    P C Buffington  RM
Kingwood
    W C Shafer    Den
Lewisburg
    H R McIlwaine  HS
Martinsburg
    C R Stribling    HS
    J M Stribling    HS
Moorefield
    H A White    HS
    R A White    HS
    George Shipley  RM

Parkersburg
    (W C Shafer    Den)
Romney
    (J B Finley    HS)
Wellsburg
    J W Cooper    Mich
    W C Jacob    WJ
    Samuel Jacob  WJ
Wheeling
    R H Devine    Beth
    J B Wilson    Beth
    A C Whitaker  Ken
    (Lewis Baker, Jr  Ste)
    R H Cummins  WJ
    C B Baguley    WJ

## WISCONSIN.

Beaver Dam
    F G Young    JH
    G A Talbert    OW
Beloit
    S R Slaymaker
        Bel and Nw
Black Earth
    H P Stoddart    Wis
Brooklyn
    C M Conradson  Wis
Clinton
    O C Olds    Bel
Columbus
    R S Rockwell    Wis
Delavan
    H D Densmore  Bel

Eau Claire
    F A Teall    Wis
Evansville
    W S Axtell    Bel
Geneva Lake
    G W Whyte    Mich
Janesville
    B G Bleasdale  Bel
    F D Jackson    Bel
Madison
    F M Brown    Wis
    C M Morris    Wis
    F W Stearns    Wis
Markesan
    J L Mitland    Wis
Menominee
    F M Stephenson  Wis

Milwaukee
    C H J Douglass  Mich
    E A Benson    Mich
    W R Smith    Wis
Monroe
    A C Copeland  Cor
    J J Schindler    Wis
Rochester
    W A Russell    Bel
Whitewater
    H S Shedd
        Bel and Wis
    C I Earll    Wis
    R C Warne    Wis
    A P Delaney    Wis
    S S Cook    Wis

## WYOMING.

Rock Springs
    J C Tisdale    Nw

## FOREIGN ADDRESSES.

| | | | |
|---|---|---|---|
| Buenos Ayres, Argentine Republic | | Middletown, New Brunswick | |
| L V P Cilley | Me | C T Vose | Me |
| Melbourne, Australia | | Truro, Nova Scotia | |
| D E Jenkins | Woos | G M Campbell | Ill |
| Vienna, Austria | | Brantford, Ontario | |
| (F H Edsall | Pa) | B B Tuttle | Dea |
| Rio de Janeiro, Brazil | | Toronto, Ontario | |
| C B Van Tuyl | Col | W E H Massey | Bos |
| Erlangen, Germany | | Charlottetown, Prince Edward Island | |
| (T B Evans | Col) | W P Taylor | Bos |
| Gottingen, Germany | | Not definitely known | |
| (W B Holcombe | Bos) | (J F Davis | Cali) and |
| Heidelberg, Germany | | (F S Lee | Ill) |
| (F W Cook, Jr | Wab) | are in Europe | |
| Hilo, Hawaii | | (R B Hellman | Cali) |
| S W Austin | Cali | is in Peru | |
| F A Lyman | WR | | |

---

| Name | | Name | | Name | |
|---|---|---|---|---|---|
| Harris, J C | Cum | Hughes, S C | Wab | Kephart, W H | Wit |
| Harris, W | Miss | Hull, F E | Me | Kern, E G | Mad |
| Harris, W C | Mich | Hume, A | Van | Kern, J W | Va |
| Harris, W M | Cor | Humphrey, C | OU | Kerr, J B | Cum |
| Harris, W W | Mich | Humphrey, H H | Cor | Kieff, J W | Wab |
| Harrison, A B | Rut | Humphreys, H | Wit | Killough, O N | Miss |
| Harrison, C W | Rut | Hunt, J E | Nw | Kilpatrick, G B | Cum |
| Harrison, W, Jr | Westm | Hunter, W | Van | Kimball, F I | Me |
| Harwood, W S | Ia | Hurd, J L | Col | Kimmel, A J | Mad |
| Hatfield, H R | Nw | Hutchinson, G W | Br | Kimmell, F M | Beth |
| Hauser, W H | Woos | Huxford, E D | Nw | Kinnear, W S | Kas |
| Hawkins, W C | Ste | Hyde, H M | Bel | Kip, W I | Cali |
| Hayden, S J | Cen | Hyde W G | OS and OU | Kirkpatrick, C | Cum |
| Heath, D L | Va | Iliff, W S | Nw | Kirkpatrick, W G | Van |
| Hector, M E | DP | Ingalls, F P | Cor | Kirkwood, S | Woos |
| Heibertshausen, F B | Wit | Ingham, G W | Ia | Kirkwood, W P | Woos |
| Hellman, R B | Cali | Insley, M H | Wab | Kitchen, E E | Den |
| Helmle, G B | SL | Irvin, C J | Pa | Knapp, A E | Mad |
| Hering, C C | RM | Irvin, F P | DP and OW | Knerr, C L | Wit |
| Herrick, C | WR | Irvine, C H | Cn | Knerr, E B | Wit |
| Herrick, H B | WR | Isaac, R M | Ste | Krecker, J P | Pa |
| Hervey, H D | Den | Israel, F S | Beth | Lake, R C | Col |
| Hess, H R | Wab | Jack, J D | WJ | Lake, W G | Dick |
| Hester W L | DP and Ind | Jackson, F D | Bel | Lampton, T B | Miss |
| Hetzler, H G | Mich | Jacob, S | WJ | Laney, J W | IaW |
| Hibbitt, R F | Van | Jacob W C | WJ | Lanier, E B | Nw |
| Hickman, S T | Cen | Jacobs, H L | Am | Lashbrooke, E L | Miss |
| Higgins, C H | OU | Jaynes, J C | Harv | Lathrop, L E | DP |
| Hight, R F | Ind | Jenkins, D E | Woos | Lauder, J M | Van |
| Hill, E P | Cum | Jenkins, J B | Harv | Laws, C L | Rich |
| Hill, H N | Ken | Johnson, A G | OU | Lawton, C E | Br |
| Hill, W R | Miss | Johnson, C E | Va | Lazell, J D | Me |
| Hinchliff, W E | Am | Johnson, D P, Jr | Ia | Leake, J J | RM |
| Hirst, C H | OS | Johnson, E L | Ia and Mich | Learned, A B | Miss and Van |
| Hobson, J S | RM | Johnson, J H | Miss | Lederle, E J | Col |
| Hodges, J R | Cum | Johnson, J M | OU | Lee, F S | JH |
| Hoe, F W | Woos | Johnston, E A | Bos | Lee, J H | Mich |
| Holcombe, W B | Bos | Jones, C | WR | Lee, L B | Mich |
| Holloway, S | Miss | Jones, F T | OW | Lees, J T | WR |
| Holmes, R E L | Va | Jones, G | Den | Leete, P | OU |
| Holt, H C | Harv | Jones, G N | Harv | Leonard, H | Ind |
| Hood, F C | Harv | Jones, H L | Den | Lewis, C C, Jr | HS |
| Hooker A W | Miss and Rich | Jones, L | Westm | Lewis, C G | Nw |
| Hoover, H C | Miss | Jones, R K, Jr | Me | Lewis, E F | Ste |
| Hopkins, A C, Jr | HS | Jones, R T | WJ | Lewis, F D | Un |
| Hopkins, W B | HS | Jones, S C | Cen and Col | Lewis, R W | Cum |
| Hough, T | JH | Jones, T T | HS | Libby, C L | Me |
| Houston, T W | Kas | Jones, W A, Jr | Col | Lillard, R H | Beth |
| Houston, W B | Cum | Judson, L E | Am | Lincoln, H F | Me |
| Howard, J H | Ind | Jungerman, C L | Van | Lincoln, M H | Pa |
| Howe, W D | Ind | Kastendieck, J T W | Un | Liotard, F F A | SL |
| Howell, H | Cali | Kastle, J H | JH | Lippincott, J B | Kas |
| Howes, C L | Me | Keener, A F | Woos | Little, W S | Bos |
| Hubbard, J B | Nw | Keller, S S | Wit | Lockwood, J F | Me |
| Hubbard, S, Jr | Cali | Kelley, J H | Van | Lodge, F T | DP |
| Hughes, F H | Ind | Kendig, H J | Den | Logan, J D | Col |
| Hughes, J F | Woos | Kennedy, T M | WR | Loper, A N | IaW |

| | | | | | | | |
|---|---|---|---|---|---|---|---|
| Percival, F R | Col and Cor | Reynolds, I W | Rut | Scott, S E | Pa |
| Perkinson, W H | Va | Reynolds, J B | Rut | Scott, W S | DP |
| Perry, W | Kas | Reynolds, J C | Dick | Seagrave, C P | Br |
| Peters, W F | Un | Rhett, H J | Br | Sears, F W | Am |
| Pettinos, G F | Dick | Rhodes, J J | Miss | Shackelford, M L | RM |
| Pfau, W H | Cor | Ribble, F W | Rut | Shaenfeld, C | Beth |
| Phelps, C D | Am | Rich, C A | SL | Shafer, W C | Den |
| Phelps, F W | Am | Rich, J M | SL | Shannon, E L | OW |
| Philbrook, W | Me | Rich, L | Nw | Shannon, J S | Ind |
| Philips, N A | Beth | Richards, C R | Bos | Sharpe, L K | Miss |
| Pickering, C C | OW | Richardson, W G | Miss | Sharpe, T S | Miss |
| Pickering, J T | OW | Riley, O B | Han | Shattuck, J C | Mich |
| Pierce, C C | Mad | Riley, W B | Han | Shaw, A R | HS |
| Pierce, E E | Br | Riley, W L | Han | Shedd, H S | Bel and Wis |
| Pittman, A L | Miss | Ritter, J C | Cum | Sheldon, F W | Cor |
| Plenkharp, C V | OS | Roberts, H A | Westm | Sheldon, J H | Ste |
| Pochler, O H | Kas | Robertson, J B | Van | Shepardson, D, Jr | Den |
| Pollard, E B | Rich | Robertson, J R | Bel | Shepardson, F W | Br |
| Pomerene, W R | OS | Robertson, J W | Bel | Shepherd, W O | DP |
| Poole, W H | Am | Robinson, G W | Kas | Sheppard, W C | Den |
| Porter, C M | Ia | Robinson, H D | SL | Sherman, F D | Mich |
| Post, W C | Ste | Robinson, W H | Un | Sherman, H T | Br |
| Powell, C E | Mich and Van | Rockwell, R S | Wis | Shick, W F | Un |
| Powers, O H | Bos | Roser, S D | Cen | Shiel, L | Br |
| Pratt, A H | Am | Ross, J B | Mich | Shipley, G | RM |
| Pratt, J L, Jr | Cor | Rowe, P | RM | Shively, H L | Cor |
| Prentiss, G F | Am | Rowlett, J W | Han | Shives, G A | Woos |
| Pretzman, C J | Wit | Roy, C D | Rich | Shumway, P R | Nw |
| Prewett, A L | Van | Rucker, J W | DP | Siebert, W H | OS |
| Price, G L | Mich | Rugg, M L | Mad | Sigmund, F L | Wit |
| Pusey, A B | Van | Ruhm, J J G | Van | Silvernail, F H | Un |
| Pusey, W A | Van | Rumble, H H | Beth | Simon, C E | JH |
| Quereau, E C | Nw | Rupert, H L | Rut | Simon, E W | Wit |
| Quick, G W | Rich | Russell, W A | Bel | Simon, J S | Wit |
| Quin, H M | Miss | Russell, W E | Am and Ken | Simpson, R L | Westm |
| Quincy, W J | Mad | Rutherford, S M | DP | Sinnott, W I | Miss |
| Rabb, A | Ind | Saal, G F | Cor | Skillman, O T | Cen |
| Radford, B S | Cum | Sabin, E H | Ia | Skinner, C | Va |
| Radliff, K C | Un | Sabine, W C | OS | Skinner, C E | OS and OU |
| Rafferty, J W | SL | Sackett, J T | Cor | Skinner, E B | OU |
| Ramage, B B | Harv | Sadler, L A | WR | Slack, H R, Jr | JH |
| Ramsdell, D H | Mich | St. Clair, F P | Beth | Slaughter, C C | Van |
| Randolph, E C | OW | St. John, W A | Mad | Slaughter, J L W | Van |
| Rank, C G | Den | Sanders, W E | Col | Slaymaker, S R | Bel and Nw |
| Rankin, R C | Kas | Sandt, G F | Ste | Snedes, E B | JH |
| Ray, I B | Me | Sargent, J A | Kas | Smith, A H | Wit |
| Raymond, C B | Am | Sargent, W H | Me | Smith, A P | Am |
| Raymund, F M | OS | Sawyer, C A | Br | Smith, C | Kas |
| Reakirt, L B | Woos | Savage, W L | Am | Smith, C F | Br |
| Reasoner, J P | DP | Scarborough, J V B | Am | Smith, C T, Jr | Rich |
| Reed, F E | Kas | Scarborough, T W | Am | Smith, E A | OW |
| Reed, G W | OU | Scarborough, W W | Am | Smith, E F | IaW |
| Reed, G W | Am | Schindler, A D | Cali | Smith, H F | Kas |
| Reed, W T | Kas | Schindler, J J | Wis | Smith, H M | SL |
| Reid, J C | Beth | Schwartz, H S | Mad | Smith, I F | Am |
| Reigart, J F | Dick | Schwill, F | Woos | Smith, J E | Am |
| Renz, G A | Pa | Scott, F M | Miss | Smith, J G | Mich |

| | | | | | | |
|---|---|---|---|---|---|
| Whitney, H A | Am | Williams, W H | Harv | Woodin, H P | Am |
| Whitthorne, H Y | Cen | Willis, G W | Br | Woods, C F | Va |
| Whitthorne, W C | Cen | Wilson, J B | Beth | Woodward, W M | Ia |
| Whyte, G W | Mich | Wilson, O G | IaW | Woodworth, H J | OS |
| Wiegand, H H | JH | Wilson, O S | Han | Woolery, L C | Beth |
| Wilbar, A E | Am | Wilson, R D | Harv | Woolson, J L | IaW |
| Wilbar, C B | Am | Wilson W H | HS | Woolson, P B | IaW |
| Wilcox, P | Col | Winfree, H L | RM | Worman, I D | Wit |
| Wilcox, W P | Col | Winfree, P B | RM | Worstell, I G | OU |
| Wilkin, J L | Den | Winfree, R | RM | Wright, A L | Beth |
| Wilkinson, G | Cali | Winslow, J R | JH | Wright, F P | Ia |
| Williams, B A | OW | Wise, H E | Ind | Wright, G S | Ia |
| Williams, C O | Br | Wise, O J | Va | Wyatt, W | Ind |
| Williams, C S | IaW | Withrow, S P | OW | Wynkoop, R B | Ken |
| Williams, C S | Me | Wolf, W H | Beth | Yocum, A D | Dick |
| Williams, E A | Den | Wood, C E | Kas | Young, F G | JH |
| Williams, H A | Wit | Wood, H G | Br | Young, F L | OW |
| Williams, H W | JH | Wood, W E | Mich | Young, J B | Nw |
| Williams, R B | Cum | Wooden, C R | IaW | Zellar, C M | DP |
| Williams, R C | Rich | Woodin, E B | Am | Zenblin, C N | Nw |
| Williams, S C | Van | | | | |

## ABBREVIATIONS.

Am.—Amherst.
Bel.—Beloit.
Beth.—Bethany.
Bos.—Boston.
Br.—Brown.
Cali. — University of California.
Cen.—Centre.
Col.—Columbia.
Cor.—Cornell.
Cum.—Cumberland.
Den.—Denison.
DP.—DePauw.
Dick.—Dickinson.
HS. — Hampden Sidney.

Han.—Hanover.
Harv.—Harvard.
Ind.—Indiana University.
Ia. — University of Iowa.
IaW - Iowa Wesleyan.
JH.—Johns Hopkins.
Kas. — University of Kansas.
Ken.—Kenyon.
Mad.—Madison.
Me.—Maine State College.
Mich.—University of Michigan.

Miss.—University of Mississippi.
Nw.—Northwestern.
OS —Ohio State University.
OU.—Ohio University.
OW —Ohio Wesleyan.
Pa. — University of Pennsylvania.
RM.—Randolph Macon.
Rich.—Richmond.
Rut.—Rutgers.
SL.—St. Lawrence.
Ste.—Stevens.

Un.—Union.
Van.—Vanderbilt.
Va. — University of Virginia.
Wab.—Wabash.
WJ.—Washington and Jefferson.
WR. — Western Reserve.
Westm.—Westminster.
Wis — University of Wisconsin.
Wit. — Wittenberg.
Woos.—Wooster.